Marxian Utopia?

A theoretical critique of Marxism
by
Neven Sesardić
and
an historical critique
by
Domenico Settembrini

Preface by
Frank Chapple

Marxian Utopia?

First published in January 1985
by
The Centre for Research into Communist Economies
c/o 2, Lord North Street, London SW1P 3LB

ISBN   0 948027 01 0

Printed in Great Britain by
Pika Print Limited, Genotin Road, Enfield, Middx. EN1 2AA

Contents

Foreword, by Ljubo Sirc   5
Preface, by Frank Chapple   7

Part One
HOW HAS MARXISM SURVIVED?
    A contribution to the critique of Marxian Utopia
    by Neven Sesardic   9
Biographical Note and Acknowledgements   10
Introduction   11

I.   From Philosophy to Science — and Back   12
    The Marxist's dilemma   13

II. The collapse of Marxist Economics   14
    Value depends on labour ...   16
    ... but labour depends on value   18
    "Labour power" and "exploitation"   20
    Why "surplus value"?   21
    The unsolved mystery of price   27
    No explanation of exchange   30
    Labour theory of value abandoned   32
    "Pauperisation" disapproved   34
    Other predictions falsified   35
    Search for a rationalisation   38

III. The Refuge of Philosophy   39
    The new orthodoxy: method not results   41

    Activism   42
    No choice of values   42
    No neutral science   44
    Marx knows best   47
    Pseudo-objectivism   50
    The Marxist "tendency"   51
    Non-Marxists cannot criticise Marxism   53

Abstractness   54
  What kind of utopia?   54
  Vagueness licenses opportunism   57
  Criticism is not prescription   58

IV. In Place of God?   60

Footnotes   61

Works cited   61

Part Two
AN ARMED PROPHESY
  From theoretical to historical critique
  by Domenico Settembrini   65
Biographical Note   66
  Why did Marxism succeed?   68
  Marxist "duplicity"   69
  Keeping up revolutionary faith   70
  Emotional appeal   73
  Violence — limited future of Marxism   74

Footnotes   75

Works cited   76

ANNEXE   77

  Party tells Chinese Marx's ideas are outdated
  (*The Times,* December 8, 1984)   77

  Chinese writer faces "purge" over article,
  by Hugh Davies in Peking, *The Daily
  Telegraph*, December 11, 1984)   78

Foreword

Neven Sesardic's critique would seem an appropriate opening for the series *Understanding Economic Systems* since all Communist governments claim that their economies are based on Marx's teachings. This study by the Zagreb lecturer has just been published in Yugoslavia, where Marxism is the official doctrine.[1] The paper is prefaced by the veteran British trade-union leader, Frank Chapple, and commented upon by the Italian specialist, Professor Domenico Settembrini, who widens Sesardic's theoretical approach into a historical critique. It is certainly remarkable that of the three contributors one was educated in a Communist country while the other two are former members of their national Communist Parties.

Since the authors find Marxism wanting, future CRCE publications will explore the question of how the doctrine has been modified to serve as a basis for working economies. In this context, it is interesting to note that the official Chinese Communist *People's Daily* has just accused ideology specialists of delaying progress. A report on the newspaper's front-page leading article, as printed recently in *The Times* is reproduced as an annexe to this Paper together with an article from *The Daily Telegraph* on the subsequent mitigation of the original statement.

The constitution of the CRCE requires that Trustees and Advisors dissociate themselves from the analyses contained in this Paper which is nevertheless commended as a unique contribution to public understanding and discussion.

Ljubo Sirc

January 1985

---

1. In *Filozofske Studije XV* (Philosophical Studies XV), the Almanack of the Serb Philosophical Society.

Preface

Marx himself is reputed to have told admirers that he did not know what a Marxist was. For their part, Marxists usually insist that Marx did not set down a body of dogma to be followed automatically, but a method of comprehending the phenomenon of nature, history, economics, politics.

Marx, however, had no practical experience to which he could refer to substantiate his theories that the collapse of capitalism would give rise to a more advanced and liberated society in which all things would be owned and controlled in the name of all the people by the state. Moreover, his collaborator and mentor, Frederick Engels, confidently foretold that following the overthrow of capitalism the state would wither away: "the government of persons is replaced by the administration of things" (*Socialism: Utopian and Scientific*).

If Marx were alive today he would be shocked at the number of so-called disciples who believe the views he expressed in 1848 relate to today's problems. Political dogma, which goes under the dubious title of Marxism, makes little sense when related to the mixed economy: for, who is the class enemy in a nationalised industry? Marxism serves mainly as justification for disgruntled elitists to perpetuate class war concepts. The tragedy is that in spite of Marx's irrelevance to modern economic and industrial problems, we have a hotch-potch of communists, trotskyists and associated groups all claiming to be true descendants of Marx. The irrelevance of their creed causes them to rig ballots, denigrate Western democracy and act as apologists for the Soviet Union and its satellites. This marks them out, not simply as dangerous idealists, but denizens of a political undergrowth that spawned fascism and applauds political dictators.

Neven Sesardic sets out, more in sorrow than in anger, the flaws in Marxist theology. When what passes for Marxism in economic theories or historical accuracy is submitted to the test of the dialectic, it is found sadly wanting. Alas, the self-proclaimed scientific socialists have their own self-perpetuating delusions to safeguard their cherished dogmas.

Having imprisoned themselves, the West's Marxist intellectuals discount, without turning a syllable, the practical experiences of Marxist, Communist, governments. Brutality towards their citizenry and incompetence in almost everything save propaganda and military developments mark them down as the most audacious frauds in the annals of government. Dr Neven Sesardic's essay is yet another warning for the West to judge deeds, not words: Lest it should happen to us.

Coming closer to reality, I once discussed with a high-ranking Party official, China's plans for the future which I exclaimed were hardly Marxist. He remarked that Karl had no experience in governing a modern state.

That discussion paralleled a more recent experience reported by Alec Nove who, at a meeting in Moscow with Soviet economic advisers to the Kremlin, commented that their proposals for improving the stagnating Soviet economy were more monetarist than Marxist; certainly Marx would not have approved of them. They replied: "Don't worry, if what we propose works, it will be Marxism".

Frank Chapple

Part I
How has Marxism survived?

A CONTRIBUTION TO THE CRITIQUE OF MARXIAN UTOPIA

Neven Sesardić

Biographical note

Sesardic was born in 1949 in Belgrade. He graduated in philosophy at the Zagreb Faculty of Philosophy in 1974 from where he also received his Ph.D. in 1982. His thesis had the title Physicalism and was published in Belgrade in 1984. At present he is a lecturer at the Department of Philosophy in Zagreb and his main interest is philosophy of natural and social sciences.

Acknowledgements

This essay first appeared in Serbo-Croat in the journal *Filozofske studije* 15 (1983), pp. 41-96. I am grateful to many of my friends for their comments and criticism of early drafts. I should like specially to acknowledge the help of Zvjezdana Dukic, Leon Kojen and Professor U. T. Place.

———

Translated by

Mary Jansen and Clare McGregor

Introduction

The vision of a just society projected into the future lies at the very centre of Marxist theory. No standpoint can continue to be described as Marxist if it does not contain, or it if rejects, the idea of a radical change in the existing state of affairs; there can be no Marxism without the idea of communism.

However, this projection of a globally different, more humane form of society, is not characteristic of Marxism alone. It is the common feature of a long tradition of utopian thinkers from Plato to Skinner. Marx himself, as well as those who continued his work, was particularly interested in presenting his vision as being essentially different from other utopias, not least from those with pronounced socialist features with which it had much in common. And indeed, there is one difference which is obvious and beyond dispute. While today the work of the so-called "utopian socialists" is practically forgotten or is considered of only historical interest, Marxism still represents a theory of foremost significance and influence on political events in a large part of the world.

Is this survival a result of fundamental differences between these two types of socialist doctrine, or is it merely a question of their having experienced a different fate for some particular reasons? This essay attempts to provide an answer.

I. FROM PHILOSOPHY TO SCIENCE — AND BACK

In his first draft of the *Civil War in France*, Marx wrote: "Although in their criticism of present-day society they have clearly described the goal of the social movement, that is, the abolition of the system of hired labour with all its economic conditions of class rule, the utopian sect founders have not found in society the material conditions for its transformation, nor in the working class, an organized and conscious force of the movement." (Marx 1962, p.557)

This is one of many characteristic passages which criticise the utopian socialists not for the goal they set themselves but for the method by which they attempted to achieve it. They were censured for being unrealistic, for naively believing that their proposals for a new social order would be accepted and turned into reality the moment the advantages inherent in this perfect and just order were recognised. According to the "classics of Marxism", the fundamental shortcoming of the theories of Cabet, Saint-Simon, Fourier and Owen was that their visions of society in the future were not based on a study of social relations and laws, but were evolved "out of the human brain" (Engels, p.4), or were "bound to run into sheer fantasies". (*ibid*.)

In contrast, Marxism from the beginning presented its projection of the future as founded on reality. It is precisely the claim that the planned "Kingdom of Freedom" is already contained in some way in the existing situation which represents perhaps the most characteristic feature of Marxist social doctrine. The arguments used in attempting to provide support and foundation for the Marxist vision of the future can essentially be divided into arguments based on *philosophy* and arguments based on *economics*. Although in the chronological evolution of Marx's thought, the philosophical basis for the utopia precedes the economic, I will discuss them in the reverse order. It seems to me that there is strong justification for such a method. The history of Marxist theory after Marx shows a picture of development diametrically opposed to the way his own thought developed. The period of scientific socialism and of insistence on economic laws and determinism preceded the period, which continues today, when Marxism is inspired more by the philosophical dimension of the *Early Works*. Thus the theoretical position in early Marxism is that of the mature Marx, while more recent Marxism is dominated by ideas of Marx's youth.

This seemingly strange fact that Marxist doctrine developed in many countries in the reverse order from that of Marx himself is, nevertheless, not difficult to explain. Marx arrived relatively early at his thesis that the source of injustice and inhumanity in the capitalist system should be sought in the sphere of economic relations, and that the proletariat has a historic mission to liberate society as a whole. However, he was not satisfied with the corroboration of his theses and tried to place them on firmer and more acceptable foundations than those afforded by his purely philosophical anthropology with its Hegelian and quasi-Hegelian categories. Thus it was that *Capital* came into being; it was written with the explicit aim of "discovering the economic law of motion" of capitalist society which "through iron necessity" leads to its collapse and to the birth of a classless society. It could be said that the entire development of Marx's thought is characterised by the desire to transfer the foundation of his utopia from the insecure and inappropriate philosophical sphere to the sphere of scientifically and empirically valid laws which leave no room for doubt or vacillation. This is how Marx described the scientific foundation of his utopia, which should have made it essentially different from the dreams of other socialist visionaries, in his article "The English Middle Class" for the *New York Daily Tribune*:

"…. though temporary defeat may await the working classes, great social and economical laws are in operation which must eventually ensure their triumph." (quoted in Kolakowski 1978, I, p.303)

However, while Marx progressed from philosophy to science in the attempt to give his social doctrine the best possible foundation, Marxism went in the reverse direction: from science to philosophy. During the Second International, and for some time afterwards, most Marxists considered the economic theory of exploitation the crowning glory of Marx's teaching. The earlier works of Marx which were available to the public at that time were considered much less interesting and the view prevailed that in the works which he wrote as a young man he had still not developed his main idea. In that period, "Marxism" and "scientific socialism" were practically synonymous.

Marxists' dilemma

The change took place at the end of the 19th century and even more at the beginning of the 20th century, when the immense methodological shortcomings and empirical difficulties of Marxist economic doctrine began to manifest themselves:

"But during the 1920s we observe a phenomenon that was scientifically much more important than revisionism had been: we find an increasing number of socialist economists — some of them quite radical in politics and not all revisionist, nor 'labourist' in the political sense — who while professing the utmost respect for Marx, nevertheless began to realise that his pure economics had become obsolete. Marxism remained their creed, and Marxist remained their allegiance, but in purely economic matters, they began to argue like non-Marxists." (Schumpeter 1954, pp.883-884)

In a situation in which the defenders of concepts contained in *Capital* were quite unable to cope with the objections raised by critics, and had finally to acknowledge that the economic basis of Marxism failed to meet rational criteria, Marxists faced a dilemma. Should they accept the consequences of defeat in the theoretical field and thus abandon Marxism, or try to transfer the stronghold of Marxism from economics to a sphere where the sharp edge of criticism was less likely to reach. Those who chose the second alternative did not need to waste any time in their quest. They simply returned to the position, which Marx himself had abandoned as unsatisfactory, of basing utopia on philosophy. Thus today too, amongst the philosophers following in Marx's footsteps the prevalent stream is that which opposes scientific socialism and which wants to transfer the focus of Marxism to philosophical anthropology. This is the current which rarely mentions terms such as "rate of profit", "differential rent", "production price" and "accumulation of capital", but where one often encounters such expressions as "alienation" and "praxis". It is important, however, to realise that philosophy as the main stronghold of utopia represents a *faute de mieux* solution. Marx had adhered to it until he found a better alternative, and Marxists returned to it when that "better" alternative got into difficulties.

Let us therefore follow the development of Marxism — from science to philosophy.

II. THE COLLAPSE OF MARXIST ECONOMICS

"... it was the dogmatic rather than the scientific element in Marxism that supported a great historic movement and blossomed into an orthodox ideology. The scientific element atrophied for science progresses by trial and error, and when it is forbidden to admit error there can be no progress."

Joan Robinson

Historical materialism reveals the exaggerated claims of Marxist economic doctrine. If the super-structure is conditional upon the economic base, as historical materialism maintains, then the explanation of economic relations contains in essence the theory of society in all its aspects. Since economics determine everything else, we can deduce knowledge about all its epiphenomena from an understanding of society's economic base.

The difficulties of this standpoint are well known. What is not well known, since it is not forthcoming, is a satisfactory answer to these difficulties from the advocates of historical materialism. It is difficult to see how one can avoid acknowledging at least a certain degree of autonomy of the cultural and ideological superstructure from the economic base, and it is practically bordering on absurdity to deny that the economic organisation of society is not sometimes affected by events of a purely political or scientific nature. Aware of this, Marxists have striven, ever since the time of Engels, to modify the paradoxical implication of a strict unidirectional causality from the economic base to other social and cultural phenomena, and they were ready to permit reversals of the direction of causal action in certain cases, such that in these cases at least the super-structure determines the base. But, as many critics have rightly observed (for instance Kolakowski 1978, I, p.364; Aron 1967, p.185; Blanshard 1966, pp.176-177), however innocent it may seem, by this simple step Marxists are in fact destroying their whole position. This *new* claim — that economic relations sometimes cause events in the sphere of politics, science and culture, and sometimes the other way round — is so innocuous that nobody would want to deny it. Instead of trying to defend the original strong and radical version of the thesis of historical materialism in the face of a lack of empirical evidence in its favour, and abandoning it when this attempt failed, Marxists have been watering it down and modifying it until nothing more than a trivial, generally acceptable and entirely uninteresting claim remained.

This strategy of weakening one's own thesis in proportion to the strength of the counter-arguments is typical of many Marxist theoreticians. It is one of the things which, from the methodological point of view, have brought Marxism into disrepute. Those who modify or adapt their theses to accommodate every new objection or counter-example succeed in placing their position beyond the reach of criticism; but in making their standpoint immune from every possible refutation in this way, they fail to realise that they are simultaneously rendering it devoid of interest. This is a phenomen we shall encounter several times in the course of this essay.

I will now discuss some of the basic difficulties with which Marxist economic theory is confronted. The main aspect of my interest will be the doctrine as presented in *Capital*. For a long time after Marx's death this aspect of the theory was regarded as the cornerstone of Marxism and no significant changes or modifications in it were felt to be necessary. In examining it I will restrict myself mainly to a discussion of so-called "classical" Marxist economics. This is for two reasons. In the first place, this part of the essay is designed to provide a *historical* analysis of a period in the development of Marxism when, in the first decades of the 20th century, the economic theory collapsed as the basis for Marx's political philosophy. In the light of this degeneration of scientific socialism,the reasons for the revival of interest in the works of the young Marx and in the so-called "re-philosophication" of Marxism become much clearer. For when the fundamental standpoint contained in *Capital* became the target of criticism to which no reply could be found, those who were still not prepared to abandon Marx's millenarian vision of the future had no choice but to seek *new* reasons for the justification of their unswerving loyalty to the ideal.

Secondly, although entirely unorthodox versions of Marxist economic theory have been evolved more recently, it is at times hard to say why they are described as "Marxist" at all. No claim is made for these revised versions of Marxist economic theory that they are designed to serve, nor indeed could they serve, as a foundation for a revolutionary political ideology. Since the intention of the first part of this essay in not to discuss Marxist economics *tout court*, but rather to present a critique of economics as a possible foundation for the Marxist utopia, it seems to me that restricting the analysis to "canonised" Marxist teaching will not diminish the general validity of my conclusions.

Value depends on labour ....?

Marx begins his analysis in the *Capital* with an attempt to determine what is common to all objects which are exchanged on the market and which can be said to have a value. He arrives surprisingly quickly and easily at the conclusion that the *only* thing common to these objects is the amount of labour embodied in them. This brief and inadequate derivation which contains virtually no argumentation would hardly convince anybody who did not already believe in the labour theory of value. The objective reader is bound to react to this in a similar way to Emile Durkheim's comment on *Capital* in his lectures on socialism:

> "How many statistical data, how many historical comparisons, how many studies would be necessary to resolve any of the numerous questions dealt with there! Is there any need to recall that a whole theory of value was established there in a few lines?" (Durkheim 1928, pp.5-6)

Thorstein Veblen was even harsher in his lecture in 1906:

Marx .... "offers no adequate proof of his labour-value theory. It is even safe to go further, and say that he offers no proof of it. The feint which occupies the opening paragraphs of the *Kapital* and the corresponding passages of *Zur Kritik*, etc., is not to be taken seriously as an attempt to prove his position on this head by the ordinary recourse to argument. It is rather a self-satisfied superior's playful mystification of those readers (critics) whose limited powers do not enable them to see that his proposition is self-evident." (quoted from: Spiegel 1952, p.180)

In fact, the simple solution Marx proposes is wrong on two counts. It is neither true that there are no other properties common to objects exchanged in the market, nor is it true that their common property is the labour invested in their production.

What is common to market objects is the fact that, for example, they satisfy some particular human need and that they are available in limited quantities only. Why not rely, for instance, on these two properties and try to evolve some kind of alternative theory of value? Marx's elimination of the use-value as a possible common property and source of value is based on a logical fallacy in his reasoning. He says:

"... the exchange relation of commodity is characterised precisely by its abstraction from their use-values. Within the exchange relation, one use-value is worth just as much as another, provided only that it is present in the appropriate quantity." (Marx 1982, vol.1, p.127)

As Boehm-Bawerk rightly noted (1921, pp.383-384, and 1975, pp.74-75), Marx confused here the abstraction from a property and the abstraction from the specific ways in which this property manifests itself. In explaining the process of commodity exchange, we can consider the specific form of the use-value of a commodity as fairly irrelevant, but it certainly does not follow from this that its having *some kind* of use-value is irrelevant. (Similarly, when we are explaining the acceleration of a body there is no need to inquire about the nature of the force that is acting on it, whether it is electro-magnetic, gravitational or some other kind; but it does not follow from this that it is irrelevant that a force of *some kind* is acting on it.)

Secondly, not all objects exchanged are a product of labour. Land, standing timber, rare objects accidentally discovered can have a large market value without any labour having been invested in them. Attempts by Marxists to deal with these direct counter-examples of their theory of value are extremely unconvincing. At the same time, it is not difficult to think of objects which are valueless even though many hours of "socially necessary labour" have been spent on their production, such as objects that are difficult to produce but satisfy no human need. Plainly an object that cannot be used to satisfy some human need has no value.

Confronted with this difficulty, Marxists try to recognise the relevance of use-value by postulating as a necessary condition for the possession of value the fact that an object must have at least some kind of use-value. But this will not meet the case since it is clear that the use-value and exchange-value are actually much more closely linked than this would suggest. The idea that is now being proposed is that the value of a commodity consists of a bare minimum which is contributed by utility, the remainder being contributed by labour *alone*. But this cannot be right, as is shown by the fact that *ceteris paribus* the value is always *proportional* to utility.

.... but labour depends on value

The next difficulty for those who see the labour invested as the primary determinant of economic value is the indisputable fact that different sorts of labour contribute to a differing extent to value. Thus five hours of labour by an unskilled worker produces a much lower value than five hours' work by a specialist. The defenders of the labour theory of value need to find a kind of labour to which all other types could be reduced and which would then serve as a common and universal measure of value.

Marx claims that all other types of labour can be reduced to unskilled or simple labour:

> "More complex labour counts only as *intensified*, or rather *multiplied* simple labour, so that a smaller quantity of complex labour is considered equal to a larger quantity of simple labour." (Marx 1982, vol.1, p.135)

It is easy to see, however, that no reduction to a common measure is achieved by saying that complex labour *counts as* simple labour. This can best be seen in the analogy put forward by Boehm-Bawerk (1921, pp.388-389). Let us assume that someone determines that the price of a railway ticket in a certain country should be dependent exclusively on the distance covered. Let us also assume that a particular stretch of track was especially difficult to build and that over this stretch the journey is twice as expensive. In such a situation, the person who established distance as the exclusive criterion for the cost of the journey could continue to adhere to his assertion and apply a method of reasoning analogous to that of Marx. He could say: 'On the said stretch of track one kilometre in fact *counts* as two ordinary (or 'simple') kilometres, and thus my initial assumption that the kilometres travelled are the only factor determining the fare is still true.'

Despite this verbal justification, it clearly recognises that there are other factors besides distance influencing the price. For one kilometre of railway does not count as two simple kilometres because it really contains these two kilometres in some way. The words "counts as" simply indicate that one kilometre of the journey on the more difficult stretch is, *for one reason or another*, twice as expensive.

How, then do we know that one kilometre on this stretch counts as two kilometres? Simply by the price! The circularity is now quite evident. First there was the attempt to find a sole criterion that would explain the prices of railway tickets, and then there was the conclusion that they depend exclusively on the distance travelled: but this distance is, at least on some stretches, measured not in metres or kilometres but by how much more it costs to travel on these sections than on other less difficult sections. In short, the following happens: the distance travelled is established as the independent factor which alone determines the cost of the journey, and how long a distance is (or how long it "counts as") is determined by reference to the cost of travelling over that stretch.

The same kind of circularity is contained in Marx's reasoning. He established the number of hours of socially necessary *simple* labour time as the common criterion for the value of all objects, believing that a given number of hours of complex labour could always be reduced to a greater (multiplied) number of hours of simple labour. It is, however, quite clear that complex labour does not "contain" simple labour in any comprehensible meaning of the word. What would it mean if we said that five hours of a skilled engineer's labour contained 10 hours of the labour of an unskilled worker? What Marx most likely had in mind is that the value of the product which a skilled engineer produces in five hours is on average the same as that of the product which an unskilled worker produces in 10 hours. However, he was then guilty of precisely the kind of circularity we encountered in the case discussed above. If the number of hours of simple labour spent is taken as that which explains the value of an object, then it is logically impermissible to refer to its value when determining how many hours of simple labour are "embodied" in a product. That Marx did in fact commit this inept *virtus dormitiva* fallacy is clearly shown by the passage in *Capital* where he explicitly refers to price in his attempt to "reduce" complex labour to simple labour. (Marx 1982, vol.1, p.305)

Some Marxists (for instance, Sweezy 1946, pp. 43-44; Rubin 1978, pp. 169-170, and Hilferding 1949, p. 146) have tried to evade Boehm-Bawerk's awkward objection by beginning to claim that what Marx really had in mind was the following: Products of complex (skilled) labour have proportionally greater value than products of simple (unskilled) labour because the value of the former not only includes the labour spent in producing them, but also all the labour which is necessary to prepare the producer for a particular skill, that is to educate him. If Marx really had in mind what such apologists, not without reason, attribute to him (Marx 1982, Vol. l, p. 273), then his reduction of complex labour to simple labour is not circular, but now contains *regressus ad in(de)finitum*. By the very nature of things both the labour of the pupil and the labour of the teacher are, as Rubin admits, spent on the process of education. But the teacher's labour *is not* simple labour and cannot be calculated by the number of hours actually spent, since the labour spent on *his* education must also be included. The same applies to the person who educates the teacher and so on *ad infinitum*. Of course, in this process the idea of the "quantity of labour" has lost any link with empirical reality, and nothing is left of the labour theory of value but its name.

"Labour power" and "exploitation"

If the law of value is valid, that is if objects are exchanged on the market at prices proportional to the labour spent on producing them, how does exploitation take place? Marx's familiar claim is that a worker is not paid for his labour, but rather that the capitalist buys his *labour-power*. This is the worker's ability to work and, like any other commodity, has its value: the number of hours of labour necessary to maintain his ability to work. Though the employer pays workers the *full value* of their labour power, he exploits them by making them work longer than would be the equivalent of the wages received and it is this *surplus value* which the capitalist keeps for himself. Thus with one (paid) part of their labour, workers earn the maintenance of their working ability, while with the other (unpaid) part they earn profit for the capitalist. (Marx was later obliged to introduce a distinction between surplus value and profit but we can disregard this in the present context.)

According to the labour theory of value, the value of labour-power as a commodity is taken to be the equivalent of what is needed to produce it; that is, to what is needed to satisfy the worker's *necessary requirements*. What are these necessary requirements? Let us see what Marx himself says about it:

"*.... the number and extent of his so-called necessary requirements*, as also the manner in which they are satisfied, are themselves *products of history*, and depend therefore to a great extent on the level of civilization attained by a country; in particular they depend on the conditions in which, and consequently on the habits and expectations with which, the class of free workers has been formed. In contrast, therefore, with the case of other commodities, the determination of the value of labour-power contains a historical and moral element." (Marx 1982, vol. 1, p. 275)

Although it seemed at first sight that the "value of labour-power" was a relatively clear and easily applicable idea, it turns out to "contain a certain historical and moral element" and depends "on the level of civilization of a country" and even on the "habits and expectations of free workers." The end result of this extreme relativity of the idea of "the value of labour-power" is that it is deprived of any empirical content. By having at their disposal this vague and poorly defined concept, the content of which can be narrowed or expanded at will, Marxists have been able to say that, regardless of the amount of a worker's wage in a given situation, it is identical to the value of his labour-power. Since necessary requirements contain a "historical and moral element," a worker will at one time satisfy his necessary requirements maintaining himself and his family at subsistence level, while at another time these requirements will also include possession of a house, the education of his children, etc. Thus we arrive at the absurd conclusion that, however much workers are paid, the Marxist thesis remains true that the wage makes it possible to satisfy *only* their necessary requirements. Such irrefutability has cost dearly because, as any elementary textbook of the philosophy of science teaches us, a theory which can explain everything, in fact explains nothing.

There is yet another interesting problem in connection with the concept of labour-power. Marx maintains that the uniqueness of labour-power as a commodity lies in the fact that its use creates a greater value than that needed for its renewal (reproduction). It is therefore the only possible source of surplus value and hence of exploitation in general. Surprisingly, Marx provides no arguments or empirical support for his thesis that labour-power is the only commodity which through consumption creates a greater value than that needed for its production. He treats this assertion as self-evident and intuitively acceptable although this is far from being the case. Strangely enough, most Marxists continue to take this claim for granted, without feeling any need to adduce some kind of justification for it. One really gets the impression that readers who have absorbed the first 50 pages or so of *Capital* and found nothing problematical or controversial, need no further argument in order to accept the remaining parts.

Why "surplus value"?

Immediately after the first volume of *Capital* was published, critics began pointing out the contradiction lying at the foundations of Marx's economic doctrine, which cannot be eliminated without abandoning some of the basic premises. This is the contradiction between the labour theory of value and the theory of surplus value. Unlike the labour theory of value which maintains that commodities are exchanged in the market at prices which are at least approximately proportional to the labour invested in their production, the inevitable consequence of the theory of surplus value is that commodities will be exchanged at prices which are, *as a rule and systematically*, different from their values (that is of labour "objectified" in them).

This consequence is arrived at in a very direct and simple way. Since the capitalist's profit is nothing other than the worker's unpaid labour, it transpires that, everything else being equal, the greater the part of a certain amount of capital expended on labour-power, the greater the profit the capitalist will realise. Expressed in Marx's vocabulary, the rate of profit is higher in branches of production with a lower organic composition of capital. (The rate of profit is the ratio between the profit realised and the total amount of capital invested in the business, while the organic composition of capital is the ratio between the constant capital invested in the means of production and the variable capital expanded in the purchase of labour.) Clearly, if Marx is right in claiming that labour is the only source of profit it follows that capitalists in labour intensive enterprises will get more profit per unit of invested capital than in the capital intensive enterprises. In reality, however, there is no evidence that capitalists in less developed and less industrialised branches are in a position which is so much more favourable than that of others.

Confronted with these facts, which clearly speak against his theory, Marx had to try to find some kind of answer and he came up with the following solution. Through competition and movement of capital from one branch of production to another, a general rate of profit is established by part of the surplus value in branches with a lower organic composition of capital flowing into branches with a higher organic composition. Through this equalization, the situation is reached whereby all capitalists draw approximately the same percentage of profit per unit of invested capital. This picture is no longer crudely at variance with reality as was the case before, but it now incorporates the contradiction (between the labour theory of value and the theory of surplus value) which has already been pointed out.

In the third volume of *Capital*, which describes the determination of a general rate of profit, Marx maintains, in direct contradiction to the theory expounded at the beginning of the first volume, that products are not exchanged at their value, but rather at their *prices of production*. The production price includes both the cost price (capital invested in means of production plus labour-cost) and the *average* profit. However, the value at which, at least approximately, products are sold if the labour theory of value holds good, should include the cost price and the surplus value (that is, *not* the average profit but the value equivalent to the surplus value invested in producing the relevant commodity for which the worker is not paid). In other words, since the equilization of the general rate of profit leads to the flow of surplus value ("objectified" in products) from one branch to another, the result is that commodities of the branches with a high organic composition of capital are as a rule sold above their real value while, in branches with a higher organic composition of capital, products are likewise *systematically* sold below their real value.

Marx was particularly concerned to prove that even after the introduction of the price of production and the modifications in the third volume of *Capital*, the law of value still remained in force.

"In whatever way prices are determined.... the law of value governs their movement in so far as reduction or increase in the labour-time needed for their production makes the price of production rise or fall....

Since it is the total value of commodities that governs the total surplus value, while this in turn governs the level of average profit and hence the general rate of profit — as a general law or as governing the fluctuations — it follows that the law of value regulates the prices of production." (Marx 1982, vol. 3, pp. 280-81)

"This clearly shows that, although the cost-prices of most commodities must differ from their values, and hence their 'costs of production' from the total quantity of labour contained in them, nevertheless those costs of production and those cost-prices are not only determined by the values of commodities, and confirm the law of value instead of contradicting it, but, moreover, that only on the foundation of value and its law the very existence of costs of production, and cost-prices can be conceived, and becomes a meaningless absurdity without that premise." (Marx 1968, p.78)

"To explain, therefore, the general nature of profits, you must start from the theorem that, on an average, commodities are sold at their real values, and that profits are derived from selling them at their values, that is, in proportion to the quantity of labour realised in them. If you cannot explain profit upon this supposition you cannot explain it at all." (Marx 1935, p. 37)

It is not difficult to discover the reasons for Marx's desperate attempt to preserve the validity of his basic analysis of the capitalist system contained in the first volume of *Capital*. It contains the quintessence of his social doctrine: the theory of exploitation. According to Marx the exploitation of workers is not a matter of fraud, theft or other blatantly illegal and immoral practises inflicted on them by the capitalists. He maintains rather that is stems directly from the fundamental organisation of the capitalist system (that is from the application of the law of value, private ownership of the means of production and the existence of free labour-power). From this in turn it follows that the injustice could not be eliminated by gradual and legal means (for instance, through parliamentary reform), but that the system should be overthrown and a completely different form of society constructed.

Marx's relatively simple and initially plausible explanation of exploitation had clear political consequences and could be used to prove the need for revolutionary changes in the direction of a communist utopia. The analysis contained in the third volume of *Capital*, on the other hand, with all its modifications, epicycles and remonstrations, clearly could not be used for this purpose. As Ronald Meek points out, no revolution would ever have been achieved if formulas with prices of production had been inscribed on the red banners. (Meek 1967, p. 104)

Having demonstrated why it was so important for Marx to claim that his analysis in the third volume of *Capital* did not invalidate the law of value, it remains for me to show to what extent his claim can be defended.

Marx tried to reconcile the *prima facie* contradiction between the first and third volume of *Capital* with the thesis that prices of production, seen individually, do indeed differ from value, but that, taken overall, the sum of the prices of production is equivalent to the sum of their values. (Marx 1982, Vol. 3, p. 273, p. 259). Boehm-Bawerk was one of the first to point out the irrevelance and inadequacy of this answer. The labour theory of value should have explained the exchange of individual objects by means of the thesis that the value of each of them is at least approximately proportional to the labour invested in their production. This theory cannot be salvaged by defending the *quite different* claim that the value of all products, taken together, is proportional to the labour spent in producing them. Even if this claim were true and made any sense, it would throw no light on the process of exchange, and yet it was precisely for this purpose that the labour theory was advanced!

I will try to illustrate Marx's error of substituting one thesis for another by means of precisely analogous invalid deduction. Let us remain in the world of capitalism and suppose that someone

claims that the number of votes gained by each individual can-
didate in an election is proportional to the financial resources
which he spent on the election campaign. When it is irrefutably
proved that there is no correlation whatsoever between success
in elections and money spent on the campaign, our man could
nevertheless decide to stick to his initial hypothesis and explain
its apparent falsification by the evidence as follows: although the
number of votes cast, seen individually, does not depend on the resources spent on the election campaign, taken as a whole, the sum
of all the votes (for all the candidates) is proportional to the total
money spent. It should be noted that even if this *new* thesis were
true (that is, if the number of people voting was dependent on
the overall intensity of the campaign), unlike the *old* thesis, it can
no longer explain electoral success in financial terms.

Let us look a bit more closely at the relations between
Marx's claims identified here as P1 and P2:

P1 = Individual products are exchanged at prices which,
each taken on its own, are approximately equivalent to the
'objectified' labour in the given product.

P2 = Individual products are exchanged at prices which,
when added up, are approximately equivalent to the total
'objectified' labour in all the products.

The first claim is much stronger and logically entails the
second, but the reverse is not true. When difficulties were encountered with P1, Marx was simply content to replace it with the
weaker claim P2, not apparently realizing that this was not such an
innocent move as he claimed. To begin with, it did away with the
possibility of explaining the process of exchange by means of the
labour theory of value since, on his own admission, the prices of
products, taken individually, do not correlate with the number of
labour hours of socially necessary labour time "embodied" in
them. This has led to the labour theory of value being abandoned
because as Samuelson (1971, p. 431) so aptly notes, the alleged
transformation of value into prices is just like the 'transformation'
when someone takes a rubber and erases an initial figure (value)
and then begins again and comes up with the correctly calculated
figure (price of production). Secondly, since Marx simply replaced
claim P1 when it got into difficulties with claim P2 which has a
lesser empirical content (that is, it follows from P1 but not   the
other way round), this move in methodological terms represented
a typical example of a degenerating theory. Characteristic of such
theories is the *content-decreasing strategy:* they cope with the
difficulties they experience not by widening and deepening comprehension but by increasingly limiting and restricting their empirical content, thus avoiding any encounter with "unpleasant"
facts.

Let us look at yet another of Marx's attempt to salvage the validity of the law of value after the introduction of the prices of production:

"…. this is always reducible to the situation that whenever too much surplus value goes into one commodity, too little goes into another, and that the divergencies from value that obtain in the production prices of commodities therefore cancel each other out. With the whole of capitalist production, it is always only in a very intricate and approximate way, as an average of perpetual fluctuations which can never be firmly fixed, that the general law prevails as the dominant tendency." (Marx 1982, Vol. 3, p. 261)

The idea is extremely simple: all products, strictly speaking, are exchanged at prices of production, but, if we disregard accidental fluctuations which cancel each other out it transpires in the end that commodities are also, after all, sold at their values.

The error in Marx's reasoning is not difficult to spot. Statistically it is permissible to ignore deviations from the mean value and to treat the average result as a fair approximation of reality only if the numerical differences between the data obtained are indeed the result of *accidental* fluctuations and not of *systematic* divergencies. In Marx's case, it is precisely the latter which applies. Divergencies of prices of production from the value of products are *not* fluctuations around the value as an average. That this is a case of systematic differences is clearly shown by the fact that commodities produced by enterprises with a higher organic composition of capital are as a rule sold above their real values, while the prices of those produced by enterprises with a lower composition are *constantly* below their values. Thus, quite contrary to Marx's claim, "the dominant tendency" is that commodities are exchanged at prices which *differ* from their values. It is entirely inaccurate to claim that "on the average" commodities are nevertheless sold at their values. In fact, this claim is no more valid that it would be to conclude from an average human life-span (60 years) and an average life-span of a hamster (two years) that people and hamsters live an average 31 years, and then justify the claim by saying that we can disregard divergencies from the mean value (- 29 in hamsters and + 29 in man) which "cancel each other out." But just as hamsters do not live for anything like 31 years, so commodities in the sense of Marx's theory are not exchanged at their values.

We can conclude therefore that despite Marx's attempts to prove the contrary, the introduction of prices of production cannot be reconciled with the truth of the law of value. During the 20th century many debates have taken place on the question whether Marx was correct in one of his weaker claims in this context, namely that the assumption that commodities are sold at their values must serve as the point of departure in order for prices of production to be calculated at all. This weaker claim by Marx is not directly relevant to this discussion, since its main theme is the aspects of his economic doctrine which were intended to legitimize his vision of the future. Despite that, I would like to draw attention to the fact that many contemporary authors have put forward strong arguments against the author of *Capital* on this account as well. They believe that prices of production are calculated quite independently from values (for example, Robinson and Napoleoni), or that in contrast to Marx's standpoint, values must be calculated from prices (Roemer), or even that Marx's idea of deriving prices from values is logically inconsistent (Steedman).

The unsolved mystery of price

The aim of the labour theory of value is to explain differences in prices by the differences in the amount of socially necessary labour time required for the production of various commodities. In order for it to have an explanatory function this theory must prove the empirical link between its two parameters (the price and the number of hours of labour spent) which must, and this is of cardinal importance, be *logically independent* of one another. Marxist political economy based on the labour theory of value has violated both of these two fundamental methodological principles at one time or another and has thus either, tacitly, made the necessary labour time logically dependant on the price itself, or not succeeded in establishing the empirical link between price and labour.

If gold is x times more expensive that iron, how does one know without reference to prices that x times more labour-time is necessary to extract gold than to extract iron? I do not believe that anybody has actually counted the number of labour-hours in either case and it is not even clear how this measuring procedure could be carried out. On the one hand, it is not a question of the number of labour-hours actually spent (which could be determined at least in principle) but rather of the "socially necessary labour-time" for which the method of calculation is not specified. On the other hand, the problem mentioned earlier of reducing "complex" labour to "simple" labour remains unsolved.

Let us assume that one day huge deposits of gold are discovered which contain twice as much of the metal than all previously known deposits put together and their exploitation is begun. Let us also assume that gold from the newly-discovered deposits is considerably more difficult to extract than is usually the case. This means that the socially necessary time for the production of gold is increased and that, in accordance with the labour theory of value, the value of gold is increased. Of course, this consequence is *reductio ad absurdum* of the theory itself because it is quite clear that with the discovery of new quantities of gold, its value cannot be increased. What would, in fact, happen in such a situation is that under the more difficult conditions it would either not be worth exploiting the new deposits or, if it were, the increased production would make the value of gold on world markets tumble. If someone answers in Marx's defence that in the example quoted the *value* of gold has indeed increased and only the price *has dropped* due to increased supply, then the second methodological rule that there must be some kind of empirical link between the *explanandum* (price) and the *explanans* (value) is violated. If disproportions between prices and values can be arbitrarily large and arbitrarily long, it is clear that, whatever values we might postulate to begin with, no imaginable movement of prices would make us abandon our initial assumption.

Unlike the first methodologically incorrect method, whereby the value of a commodity was determined by taking into consideration its price (in other words, precisely what it should have explained), what is methodologically wrong with the second method is that the values of commodities are now defined in such a way that it is quite irrelevant what happens to prices (again precisely what they should explain). A good example of this second error is to be found in Hilferding's attempt to reply to Boehm-Bawerk's critique of Marx:

> "Boehm-Bawerk's mistake is that he confuses value with price, being led into this confusion by his own theory. Only if value (disregarding chance deviations, which may be neglected because they are mutually compensatory) were identical with price, would a permanent deviation of the prices of individual commodities from their values be a contradiction to the law of value." (Hilferding 1949, p. 156)

In Hilferding's view even the discrepancy between values and prices which remains, after the "chance deviations" which are mutually "compensatory" will not dispute the validity of the law of value. But we have to ask ourselves, on what basis this law is valid if there is no link whatsoever between the commodity price and its value.

Let us examine this more closely. The labour theory of value contains three fundamental concepts: value, labour and price. The relation between the first two is logical because the value is defined as objectified labour. This definition, taken on its own, is an arbitrary linguistic convention which as yet contains no information at all about the economic sphere and which cannot therefore be the subject of a meaningful discussion.

As G.D.H. Cole said,

> "there is no way of either proving or disproving the contention that labour is the only source of 'value' if 'value' means simply that of which labour is the source" (Cole 1961, p. 287)

Joan Robinson also says something very similar:

> "Marx uses his analytical apparatus to emphasise the view that only labour is productive. In itself, this is nothing but a verbal point. Land and capital produce no *value*, for *value* is the product of labour-time." (Robinson 1966, pp. 17-18)

To arrive at an economic theory, the third concept (price) has to be introduced in such a way as to link somehow empirically with the first two. Until a certain empirical link between prices and values has been indicated, we are dealing with an arbitrary definition rather than an economic theory whose tenability we can begin to discuss.

We see now the weakness of Hilferding's defence of Marx's doctrine. Boehm-Bawerk has not "confused" value and price, as Hilferding thinks, but has adopted the only method by which the labour theory of value can be disputed, namely by indicating the absence of any empirical inter-dependence of prices and values. Hilferding, on the contrary, believes that though there really is no agreement between prices and values, this does not constitute a challenge to Marx's theory of value. In so doing he has actually reduced the theory to a trivial and, by definition, true assertion ("value = objectified labour") which does not claim to say anything about prices or the actual process of exchange.

What does stick out like a sore thumb in classical Marxist economic teaching is the lack of readiness on the part of his followers to put forward any kind of concrete and clear claim about the nature of the link between prices and "objectified" labour. If, however, we reject the methodologically invalid formulations of the labour theory of value, we must conclude that while they fail to state any kind of contingent link between prices and labour which could be subjected to empirical test, Marxists are not putting forward a theory but merely a set of claims which look like a theory.

It is futile to try and remedy the matter, as do Marx (1982, Vol.1, p. 260) and Hilferding (*loc. cit.*) by resorting to the thesis that value determines prices *in the final analysis*. For when this expression "in the final analysis" is examined, it boils down to a mere assurance that the link between prices and values does exist although it has not yet been discovered. By using this magic formula, Marxists need no longer concern themselves with possible discord between their theory and the relevant empirical facts, because they can now answer any such objection even before they have heard it in full. Their answer to any discrepancy between prices and "objectified" labour, no matter how extreme, will be that they never believed that this was a question of "direct" agreement, but was only "in the final analysis".

No explanation of exchange

Marx's theory of value, as Ronald Meek correctly notes, "has crystallised a basic methodological principle — the principle that conditions of exchange should properly be analysed in terms of conditions of production" (Meek 1977, p. 124). Although it might appear that this methodological principle represents an entirely natural way of explaining the process of exchange to which there can be no objection, I shall try to demonstrate how this point of departure leads to a fundamentally erroneous strategy of research.

To this end it is necessary, first, to point out the crucial difference between the two types of explanation and two types of explanatory relationship in which two phenomena or two types of phenomena can stand with respect to one another. The two types of explanation are respectively *genetic explanations* and *functional explanations*, while the relationship is that of being genetically or functionally explanatory the one of the other. In terms of this distinction a phenomenon A is said to be genetically explanatory of another phenomenon B if A explains how system B came into existence and acquired the properties it has. Such an explanation cannot be expected to explain how system B works, what it is about its make-up that gives it those properties. For that we require a functional explanation in terms of the properties of the constituents of the system and their relation to one another. For example, describing the production process can explain the genesis of a television set but cannot explain how it functions. An investigation of the production process is genetically explanatory of the existence of the set and its properties. It can explain why the television set has the structure it has, but it cannot explain the principle on which it works. To achieve the latter, we have to refer to the physical properties of the parts of the set and their mutual relations which together provide us with a functional explanation of how the set works.

It is easy to see that the behaviour of a system can only be influenced by the properties it and its parts have at a given moment and that, apart from their role in giving the system these properties, its past and genesis no longer have any continuing causal influence. If two systems reach a completely identical situation by totally different causal paths, they will behave identically; since presumably they bear no "trace" of their different pasts, that is, since all the properties they have are common to both, there is nothing in their constitution which could cause them to behave differently.

Thus we see that although a genetic explanation of the properties of a given system can tell us how it acquired those properties, in order to explain what it is about its *present* constitution that gives it those properties this investigation needs to be replaced by an approach which pays attention exclusively to the functional properties of the parts of the system.

Armed with this distinction, let us return to Marx. His methodological principle, which requires that the process of exchange should be explained by reference to the labour which takes place in the sphere of production, amounts to an attempt to explain the functioning of the market by means of factors which are genetically explanatory and *not* functionally explanatory. In contrast to Marx's standpoint, we have to conclude in the light of this distinction that the only things which can contribute to an explanation of the exchange of commodities are the properties of the market situation as it exists *now* (the quantity of certain products, their quality, demand, etc). A genetic explanation of how a commodity acquired those properties cannot possibly hope to do the job of explaining what it is that gives the commodity those properties in the here and now.

To avoid misunderstanding, it is clear that until something is produced it cannot be exchanged. But it is also clear that it was not the aim of Marx's economic theory to "discover" this trivial truth which nobody would deny. It had much greater pretensions — not merely to demonstrate the *causal* dependence of the genesis of the market situation on the situation in production, but also *to explain* movements on the market by means of certain facts drawn from the sphere of production. The attempt to achieve this was, however, by the very nature of things, doomed to failure because the labour-process in production is not functionally explanatory in relation to the sphere of exchange. The functioning of the market is determined only by the situation prevailing at a given point in time, regardless of how it came about. Just as television sets of the same structure function identically regardless of the fact that they were assembled in different ways, so markets with the same properties (selection, quality and quantity of products, buyers' interests, etc.) function in the same way, regardless of the possibly very different types of production preceding them. Thus, analysing market phenomena by reference to the labour-process in production, which is the essence of Marx's economic approach, is simply an attempt to explain exchange with the help of parameters which are, precisely *at the level of explanation*, irrelevant to it.

On what basis are certain relations and ratios of exchange between different products on the market established? The only possible basis is the global situation at a given moment and not some perhaps distant past which belongs to the phase of production. Commodities do not bear labels stating how they were produced and how much labour was expended on them. It is therefore impossible for their "genesis" to exert an influence on their status on the market. If some commodity were to reach the market without having been produced by labour but rather created secretly *ex nihilo* and without any effort by some magician, its position in exchange would not change at all. If all the objective properties of this product remained the same how could its "historical oddity" be recognised on the market?

What made Marx's fairly implausible idea of explaining exchange with production to some extent plausible was the unfortunate and often repeated terminology he uses when speaking of "objectified labour" and of labour "embodied in a commodity". However, no labour is embodied in a commodity in any intelligible sense. The work has only been carried out beforehand, before the commodity acquired its final form. When the process of production is completed, the objects no longer bear any marks of the labour spent on them. Thus, in the process of exchange what belongs to the past and has left no specific trace can no longer be causally effective. Thereafter it is only the properties which objects now have which are causally effective. Marx's *Capital* in fact establishes a new commodity fetishism according to which some circumstances of the past history of an article continue to act causally in a mysterious and inexplicable way despite the fact that in the existing properties of the articles no trace of its past has been preserved.

Labour theory of value abandoned by Marxists

Many Marxist theoreticians who seriously concern themselves with the economy have been forced to admit that there are significant difficulties in the foundations of Marx's theory of value. Having made this concession, they could hardly agree with James Becker that the contemporary lack of interest in the labour theory of value remains something of a mystery (Becker 1977, p. 127) and can only be explained by the ideological limitations of bourgeois economists (*ibid.*, p. 157). More sensible Marxists have realised that Marx's labour theory of value can scarcely be defended as an empirical theory which is supposed to explain social phenomena. So they have either tried, like Roemer (1982, pp. 150-151 and pp. 287-288), to present this theory as a consequence of the teachings on the class struggle, or maintained that it is only a "parable" (Bose 1975 pp. 141-145) which is meant to prove the fact of exploitation and afterwards be rejected! Others again, like

Steedman (1977, p. 162), Cohen (1979, pp. 338-360), Morishima (1973, p. 8 and pp. 193-194) and Meek (1977, p. 131), simply concluded that the time has come to reject the labour theory of value and for Marxists, as Meek says, to "face grim realities".

I will quote just two such characteristic attitudes:

"For a thorough-going Marxist it would be impossible to conceive of Marxian economics without the labour theory of value. Since it provides the workers with an inspiring ideological rationale for their struggle against bourgeois regimes, Marxists would be greatly depressed by losing its authority.... However, the most important task is of course to strengthen the foundations, for it is useless to build a palatial mansion on sand. One of the conclusions of this book is that Marx's economics can acquire citizenship in contemporary economic theory by detaching it from its roots, the labour theory of value...." (Morishima 1973, pp. 193-194)

"Marxists should therefore concentrate on developing the materialist account of why production conditions and real wages are what they are, leaving the discussion of 'value magnitude' to those concerned only with the development of the new Gnosticism." (Steedman 1977, p. 162)

It is important to understand that in this way Marx's basic idea of founding the theory of exploitation, class struggle and emergence of a communist society on the labour theory of value has in fact been completely abandoned. Many contemporary writers agree that this had, in fact, been his central idea (for example: Robinson 1964, pp. 38-39; Lange 1970, p. 228; Meek 1977, p. 132; Schumpeter 1954, p. 650; Napoleoni 1974, pp. 208-210; Samuelson 1966, p. 1511; Sik 1972, p. 130; Morishima 1973, pp. 193-194; Wolfe 1967, p. 319). According to Marx's doctrine expounded in *Capital*, exploitation is not a result of fraud, violation of norms or theft, but rather is incorporated in the principle upon which capitalist society functions. Articles are exchanged at their values and nobody can realise profit by systematically selling his products above their values or by buying somebody else's products below their true values; but exploitation remains because workers do not receive the equivalent to their labour but the equivalent to their labour-power — the only commodity which they possess and which they can market.

If the workers' position of inequality stemmed from some political injustice or accidental social circumstances, one could try to improve such a state of affairs by reforms or parliamentary means. But if exploitation is not a marginal phenomenon but a necessary and integral part of the logic of the capitalist system (as Marx maintains), then there is no way of abolishing injustice other than totally destroying this system and building *a completely new and radically different* form of society. This clearly shows how, if one accepts Marx's theory of value, it is easy to deduce the need for global and radical social change. It is, therefore, not surprising that in Marxist tradition, the economic doctrine has often been used as a way of legitimising utopia. However, we must then also understand that the failure of the labour theory of value cannot remain confined to the economic sphere, but that must at least to some extent also shake the foundations of the Marxian vision of the future.

The methodological shortcomings of the labour theory of value and of the theory of surplus value are so serious that it is very difficult today to defend Marx's original stand in a rational way. Marxists who reject these theories should not deceive themselves that their rejection is harmless when it could deeply reflect on the status and defensibility of their political philosophy.

"Pauperisation" disproved

It follows from the economic analysis in *Capital* that the working class will become increasingly impoverished. This so-called "theory of pauperisation" is in direct contrast to historical development. On average real wages are now more than four times as high as in the mid-1870 (Howard & King 1975, p. 132). Discussing the fate of Marx's prediction that the working class will become increasingly impoverished, J.R. Campbell said:

"I live in a typical London working-class suburb, and my neighbours are typical London working-class people. If these neighbours of mine are the end-product of a long historical process of 'impoverishment', then all I can say is that their grandfathers and their great-grandfathers must have been bloody rich men." (Quoted by Meek 1967, p. 123)

What is most interesting in all this is that this prediction was inaccurate even in Marx's time. Bertram Wolfe has revealingly pointed out that the detailed and careful statistical data about all possible aspects of the economic situation which Marx put forward in his main work are entirely lacking in figures about the trend in workers' wages after 1850. Bearing in mind Marx's pedantry and his undeniable knowledge of economic literature, it is difficult to explain this important omission as accidental. The fact that Marx did not mention this information, which he must have known and which contradicted his theory, led Wolfe to comment laconically: "That silence speaks louder than words." (Wolfe 1967, p. 323).

Some Marxists have tried to look for a way out by claiming that Marx was not thinking of the absolute but relative pauperisation of workers. This means that although daily wages are on the increase, the proletariat is nevertheless increasingly exploited. Here we can easily discern the manoeuvre which we have already frequently encountered, namely that if the facts refute Marx's theory it is modified in such a way as to reduce its empirical content and thus avoid its invalidation (*content-decreasing strategy*). Moreover, if Marx had really predicted the so-called "relative impoverishment," he would, as Joan Robinson so wittily observes (1965, p. 155), have written in his *Manifesto of the Communist Party*: "Proletarians have nothing to lose but the prospect of a suburban home and a motor car." We must agree that this would not have been a particularly inspiring slogan.

If anyone thinks it not entirely fair to refer to the *Manifesto* when criticising Marx's mature economic doctrine, perhaps the following quotation from his paper entitled "Value, Price and Profit" (read at sessions of the General Council of the International Workers' Association in mid-1865) will dispel doubts about whether Marx really had absolute pauperisation in mind in his predictions.

"These few hints will suffice to show that the very development of modern industry must progressively turn the scale in favour of the capitalist against the working man, and that consequently the general tendency of capitalistic production is not to raise but to sink the average standard of wages, or to push the *value of labour* more or less to its *minimum limit*." (Marx 1935, p. 61 — italics in the original)

The fate of the prediction, based on the theory of pauperisation, that precisely because of continual worsening of its position the proletariat will have the historical mission of liberating all of society and carrying out the revolution is also quite interesting. It became clear that, in the countries with the most developed capitalist systems workers were showing growing interest in the reformist movement and in the parliamentary struggle for political rights and the improvement of their living conditions, and less and less interest in a radical change in society. The explanation worked out by Lenin (1953, p. 233) was that workers are not conscious of their historical mission and that this consciousness must be "brought to them from without." Thus we see that when a conflict arises between the Marxist theory of the proletariat and the way workers behave, what needs to be corrected is not Marx's theory but the behaviour of people which does not conform to the predictions of the theory.

Other predictions falsified

There have been other unsuccessful predictions which have tormented the advocates of scientific socialism. Werner Sombart (1908, pp. 83-86 and pp. 93-96) pointed out that statistical records on the economic situation at the end of the 19th and the beginning of the 20th century did not accord with the predictions of Marx's theory of concentration (that pre-capitalist economic forms would disappear and only large enterprises remain) or the theory of accumulation (that the number of capitalist magnates would constantly decrease). Marx's conclusion, drawn from his "laws of capitalism", about the increasingly frequent emergence of crises in capitalism (Marx 1982, Vol. 1, p. 2) was also contradicted by the subsequent course of events.

One of Marx's most famous and significant predictions was the inevitable collapse of capitalism: "The knell of capitalist private property sounds. The expropriators are expropriated." (Marx 1982, Vol 1, p. 929). There is no doubt that Marx saw this as a matter of the immediate future because in some of his works (*The Poverty of Philosophy*, *Herr Vogt* and *Manifesto of the Communist Party*) he spoke of the revolutionary events which "are going on before our own eyes." His expectation of the imminent collapse of capitalism is also born out by the following words in his letter to Engels written as he was completing the *Grundrisse*:

"I am working madly through the nights on a synthesis of my economic studies so that, before the deluge, I shall at least have the outlines clear." (McLellan 1973, p. 290)

And later, during the transition from the 19th to the 20th century, Marxists were obsessed with this apocalyptic vision of the collapse of capitalist society. As Camus said:

"The revolutionary movement at the end of the 19th and the beginning of the 20th century lived, like the early Christians, in anticipation of the end of the world and the Parousia of the proletarian Christ." (Camus 1951, p. 252)

Even if we assume that the Parousia came about in 1917 (albeit further to the East then originally predicted), the fact still remains that the basic prediction did not come true: the system in which private property is legalised has survived until this day.

Marx believed that he had discovered laws which at long last explained the principle on which the capitalist system functioned, and it was from these laws that he also derived his main predictions. When they did not come true, the most natural thing to do was to conclude that there was something wrong with his theory. The only link between an empirical theory and its object lies in the fact that, as Popper (1959) observed long ago, erroneous predictions to some extent cast doubt on a theory and lead to its re-examination. If this link is broken, we are left only with *specious* empirical theories.

Some Marxists, in fact, broke this sole surviving link between

Marx's theory and economic reality by minimising the significance of the erroneous predictions in the attempt to defend it against criticism. They claimed that the failure of the predictions contained in *Capital* did not indicate that Marx's theory was wrong, only that some fresh circumstances had emerged which exerted a crucial influence on the subsequent development of events and which Marx, at his time, was unable to take into consideration. This attitude very quickly turned into a general strategy of retaining Marx's fundamental standpoints and explaining everything which did not fit into the scheme of things by the specific factors of the situation. This meant that Marxist theory was no longer required to, and was consequently no longer able to, adapt to the facts because its basic regulating mechanism had stopped working. Incorrect predictions no longer signalled that something was wrong with the theory.

Naturally, when things are done this way, the outcome which followed was to be expected. Blaug described it concisely when he said:

"Marxist economics began badly to 'degenerate' in the first decade of this century when the German Marxists failed to respond creatively to Bernstein's revisionism, and has continued to 'degenerate' ever since, the unmistakable signs of which are endless regurgitation of the same materials, the continual substitution of appeals to authority for analysis, and a persistently negative attitude to empirical research." (Blaug 1976, p. 167)

The entire methodological analysis of Marx's economic doctrine expounded earlier demonstrated that the theory had been built on unreliable foundations and had so many serious shortcomings that it was not surprising it could not go on developing and improving but was steadily heading in the direction of an increasing loss of explanatory power and empirical relevance in general. When at the beginning of this century the economic and scientific foundations of Marx's position began to crumble, it became clear that any fundamental difference between his utopia and that of the "utopian socialists" had been lost. The economic analysis presented in *Capital* should have demonstrated the essential advantage of the Marxist utopia over the unrealistic visions of Cabet, Owen and Fourier. However, instead of proving that the Marxian utopia was founded on reality, this economic analysis showed itself to be so methodologically defective that it was in fact difficult to apply to reality, and where this *was* possible, the analysis was shown to be erroneous.

The failure of scientific socialism has presented Marxists with a dilemma. Should they reject only the economic arguments and try to replace them with something else, or should they conclude that the failure to provide scientific foundations has also discredited the utopia itself as an arbitrary and unfounded vision of the future. Sombart described this historical moment of crisis in a similar way:

"The realisation that many of Marx's theories do not correspond to science, that they are false was bound to give rise to grave conflicts in the minds of orthodox socialists who were at the same time Marxists. At first an attempt was made to silence the criticism by interpreting Marx differently or by using artificial interpretations of suspect passages. But this was to no avail. In the end it had to be admitted that Marx was wrong on the most fundamental points. Now the orthodox Marxist found himself in the same position as the orthodox Christian when natural sciences undermined the foundations on which the Bible was based. He faced a dilemma; either to abandon his faith, which was cloaked in forms which science had demolished, or disregard scientific knowledge and thus save his faith." (Sombart 1908, p. 98)

The adoption of different orientations in the situation referred to had far-reaching consequences and led to a major split — a division of socialists into reformists (gradualists) and revolutionists (catastrophists). Reformists believed that the failure of Marxist economic doctrine must also reflect on the status of the Marxist utopia, for which the doctrine should have provided a foundation. It was their view that, following the failure of scientific socialism, Marx's over-ambitious and unrealisable programme of providing a scientific proof of the need for and the desirability of a global and radical change in the social system should be abandoned. It was felt that instead they should aim at bringing the socialist idea closer to reality by presenting proposals for specific measures to bring about a gradual change in social relations. A programme of detailed reforms in a spirit of socialism should be prepared, which would win the largest possible number of followers and thus have a real chance of being implemented. The reformists did not have the missionary conviction that they were the saviours of mankind and witnesses to a Truth revealed only to them, which is usually associated with intolerance and resort to undemocratic means in the struggle against political opposition. They interpreted their movement as an attempt to carry the programme of reform to victory through parliamentary struggle and compromises with the followers of other programmes and parties whose legitimacy they fully recognised.

Search for a rationalisation

Others were not inclined to take this road and give up Marx's vision of the "Kingdom of Freedom". The appalling difficulties encountered by his attempt to place this on scientific foundations did not, in their view, cast any doubt on the Marxian utopia itself. The task was simply to find new foundations to replace those which had not withstood the test of time and the confrontation with reality. A rationalisation had to be found for their belief, which remained untouched by the manifest failure of scientific socialism. The most natural thing in these circumstances was to resort to philosophy, which had earlier served as the main bastion on which Marx himself based his vision of the future. This is why the development of contemporary Marxism has been marked by a constant reiteration of the *philosophical* dimension of Marx's thought and by shifting the focus away from the later economic thories onto his early writings. The abandonment of the master's doctrine which was no longer credible and retreating to his earlier positions which could not be so easily refuted, represents in Ernest Gellner's witty formulation the tactics of *reculer pour mieux croire*. (Gellner 1974, p. 194)

II. THE REFUGE OF PHILOSOPHY

"... this impatient philosophy which aims at creating a new world without sufficient preparation in the opinions and feelings of ordinary men and women.
Bertrand Russell

The new Marxists found their basic inspiration in the "soteriology of alienation" and they tried to prove that Marx's fundamental ideas are contained in *Early Works* and not in *Capital*. This makes it difficult for them to explain why, in his lifetime, Marx was not interested in publishing the "Economic and Philosophic Manuscripts", if they indeed contained the quintessence of his philosophy. They have also tried to clear Marx of any responsibility for the application of dialectic to nature and for Engels' naive philosophy of science. They, therefore, do not like to mention the fact that Marx spoke very favourably about *Anti-Duehring*, and that in *Capital* he had advocated the applicability of the dialectic laws to nature and illustrated it with the validity of the law of transition of quantity into quality in the molecular theory of modern chemistry!

The more sensible of them had to admit that Marx obviously did not have a high opinion of his early works, and that such a strong demarcation line cannot be drawn between the thoughts of Marx and Engels.. In rejecting scientific socialism and dialectical materialism, they were aware that they were not following exactly in Marx's footsteps and they had to pretend to understand Marx better than he understood himself. (Habermas 1971, p. 244) From a logical viewpoint there can be no objection, although it sounds rather odd to claim you understand the philosopher better than he understood himself, when at the same time you regard him as the greatest thinker in history.

There is, however, a much more serious difficulty for the new Marxists. They continue to use many terms which, if one rejects the foundations of scientific socialism, no longer make any sense. For instance, in contemporary Marxist discussions reference is often made to exploitation, but the theory of exploitation is based on Marx's criticism of political economy, which we have already shown to be unfounded. Anyone who uses the category of exploitation today cannot ignore all the objections since the end of the 19th century, which have pointed to the untenability of the analysis put forward in *Capital.* If he wants to legitimise his usage of this extremely controversial concept, he must not restrict himself to speaking about alienation, human nature and praxis, but must make every effort to rehabilitate Marx's *economic* doctrine without which the category of exploitation makes no sense. Otherwise, all the critical comments directed at the labour theory of value and the theory of surplus value hold good, and on this basis we have no choice but to agree with Nozick that

"Marxian exploitation is the exploitation of people's lack of understanding of economics" (Nozick 1974, p. 262)

Another major question is whether there is any sense in talking about the contradictions of capitalist society. Marx's use of the word "contradiction" was justified in so far as he thought he had proved that this system of production was permeated by irreconcilable opposing tendencies which would inevitably lead to its collapse. If we abandon this apocalyptic vision and admit, as is very often admitted in contemporary Marxism, that capitalism has found a way of postponing its collapse for an indefinite period by making modifications, talk of the contradictions within capitalism becomes superfluous. Having learned their lesson from the ignominious fate of Marx's prophecies, contemporary Marxists are cagey about making any specific predictions. What they do not seem to see is that by making no predictions about the collapse of capitalism, whose accuracy can be tested in the light of what actually happens, the claim that the conflicts and opposing tendencies within capitalism are *irreconcilable* has been abandoned. All that is left is the trivial and generally acceptable thesis that capitalism, like any other system, is characterised by conflicts and opposing tendencies.

What is revealing is the reaction of the new Marxists to

Marx's erroneous predictions. Let us look at Lukacs's characteristic deliberations on this problem:

"Let us assume for the sake of argument that recent research has disproved once and for all every one of Marx's individual theses. Even if this were to be proved, every serious 'orthodox' Marxist would still be able to accept all such modern findings without reservations and hence dismiss all of Marx's theses in toto — without having to renounce his orthodoxy for a single moment. Orthodox Marxism, therefore, does not imply the uncritical acceptance of the results of Marx's investigations. It is not the 'belief' in this or that thesis, nor the exegesis of a 'sacred' book. On the contrary, orthodoxy refers exclusively to *method*. It is the scientific conviction that dialectical materialism is the road to truth and that its methods can be developed, expanded and deepened only along the lines laid down by its founders. It is the conviction, moreover, that all attempts to surpass or 'improve' it have led and must lead to over-simplification, triviality and eclecticism." (Lukacs 1971, p. 1)

It is interesting that Lukacs, in his second preface to *History and Class Consciousness*, 1967, singled out precisely this definition of orthodoxy as something which was "not only objectively correct but could today, on the eve of the renaissance of Marxism, also be of great significance".

The new orthodoxy: method not results

Let us analyze these propositions in greater detail. The "orthodox Marxist" is not worried in the least about Marx's incorrect predictions because his orthodoxy relates exclusively to method. It is completely unclear why he is so sure that he has discovered "the right method of investigation" when he concedes the possibility that all the results obtained by this method may be wrong. We have to conclude that the orthodox Marxist does not have a blind belief in one or the other of Marx's theses but that *he does have* a blind belief in his method.

Let us turn our attention to the sophisticated way in which Lukacs tries to present the theoretician's virtues as defects and *vice versa*. It might be thought that a demonstration that individual theses contained in a theory are false should cast doubt on the method by which these theses were arrived at in the first place. If someone is prompted to re-examine his own method of investigation as a result of the failure of his predictions, he demonstrates a laudable critical attitude towards the methodology adopted. It is not true, as Lukacs tries to suggest, that by so doing he is fated to end in "over-simplification, triviality and eclecticism". On the contrary, an orthodox Marxist is one who manifests a fundamentally irrational attitude because he admits that he will adhere to his method regardless of the results to which it leads him. Such an attitude, needless to say, it not open to rational discussion.

There is something symbolic in the fact that such overt dogmatism is proclaimed in *History and Class Consciousness*, a work which is generally held to represent the dawn of the new Marxism. This dogmatic attitude is the one common and perhaps most distinctive characteristic of all the later followers of neo-Marxism — the firm resolve to retain Marx's vision of the future as an ideal, despite the questionable nature of many of his individual theses. Since in such a short paper I cannot enter into the often subtle differences between the adherents to this movement, I will try to examine critically two aspects which, in my view, contain what is most representative of this philosophy: activism and abstractness.

ACTIVISM

Marx's 11th Thesis on Feuerbach (not published in his lifetime!) is probably the sentence most frequently quoted by his contemporary followers as containing the principle of activism:

"The philosophers have only interpreted the world, in various ways, the point, however, is to change it."

What neo-Marxists are demanding, therefore, is that philosophers should not restrict themselves to explaining and theorising, but that they should commit themselves to changes in social reality, with the aim of achieving the 'Kingdom of Freedom'. I will point out some serious difficulties which cast doubt on the justification of this aspiration to "transcend the contemplative attitude".

No choice of values

It is usually believed that if someone commits himself to implementing a certain goal, this goal appears desirable to him in the light of certain values which he attaches to it. As there are many different things to which people attach value, they set themselves different goals and ideals, and it is in the freedom to adopt and pursue these different goals and ideals that individual choice and freedom consist. Many thinkers have maintained that the judgement of an individual about what he believes to be of value is sacred, and if a fundamental dispute about values should arise it cannot be resolved rationally. It is this recognition of autonomy with respect to values which constitutes the basic principle of the liberal-democratic tradition, namely that mentally healthy adults have the right to choose their goals for themselves and decide on the way of life most acceptable to them.

The activism of the new Marxists cannot be reconciled with recognition of the individual's autonomy in the sphere of values. They *do not* present Marx's utopia as an ideal, the advantages of which are identical with what most people believe to be the best social system, but as a vision of the future, the acceptability of which stems from its being founded on philosophical comprehension. In other words, in advocating the realisation of their utopia, they are not drawing on the values and aspirations of individuals but on Marx's writings.

This also gives rise to the unusually frequent practice of passing with surprising ease over everything that *real* people desire and respect and of describing all this as "false needs" (Marcuse 1972, pp. 19-20), "false consciousness" (Lukacs 1971, p. 50), "distorted satisfaction of needs" (Habermas 1971, p. 235) and "accidental emotions divorced from real intentions and wants" (Horkheimer 1974, p. 47). The concept of alienation is also often used to discount as illusory the desires which Marxist visionaries condemn: they are not "real", "authentic" desires, but merely a result of contemporary man's "alienation".

Many philosophers, politicians and moralists have exerted a salutary influence on people by persuading them to accept new values of which our civilization today is proud. Surely there can be no objection to this desire to contribute to moral improvement and the development of higher values. However, a major and crucial difference is whether an attempt is made to pursuade by appealing to people's consciousness while constantly and absolutely respecting their values, or by the "teacher'" claiming to know better what a man's desires are or ought to be than the man himself. It is precisely this second, paternalistic, attitude which is characteristic of the new Marxists. They firmly reject the role of moralist and educator and try to prove that their knowledge of "true" values stems from this comprehension of the human essence contained mainly in the *Early Works*. They do not, therefore, present this contribution of theirs in terms of a *proposal* of new values but as a *discovery* backed by philosophical arguments.

While we can reject a proposal we do not like, we cannot do the same thing with a discovery because this would be to act entirely irrationally. If it is true that "what man really is" and "needs" were discovered in the mid-19th century, then as individuals we no longer have any freedom to choose our goals and ideals: because of various "distorting" factors, we can only be mistaken about and unaware of our "genuine" needs and goals. The neo-Marxists' position involves the following considerable paradox: a man wishing to learn what he really desires need not deliberate over his future, but simply read the "Economic and Philosophic Manuscripts."

Extensive deliberations are not necessary to grasp the dangers inherent in disregarding the views of individuals when it comes to determining their "true" needs and interests. Even the greatest injustices and crimes can be justified by claiming that such actions are carried out "for the well-being" of the victims themselves. Bukharin's "theoretical" justification of "war communism" may serve as a warning of how small the step is from the philosophy of "true" and "false" needs and interests to a cynical defence of violence:

> "Since the peasants need a strong workers' state to protect them from landowners, the fact that the Bolshevik government forcibly takes food away from them is 'objectively' in their own interests!"

Bukharin went even further when he claimed in *The Economy of the Transitional Period* that "proletarian coercion in all its forms, from death by firing squad to forced labour, represents, no matter how paradoxical this may seem, *a method of building communist mankind from the human material of the capitalist era.*" This method of re-shaping "human material" by means of forced labour and death by firing squad did not, however, appear so "paradoxical" to everyone. Lenin, for instance, noted alongside Bukharin's above sentence "Just so", while his comment on the whole chapter was "brilliant."

No neutral science

The division into value and factual judgements is a very frequent target of attacks by contemporary Marxists. Accordingly, they criticise very severely the thesis about the value-neutrality of science. For instance:

> "These late apologists of value-neutrality laud the subaltern role of thought which because of its doubtful fate now only carries out the duty of a factotum of industrial society... Scientists, on the other hand, declare that obedience is purity, scholarly strictness and such like, like citizens of a bad state who describe their silent suffering of tyranny as faithfulness and loyalty." (Horkheimer 1968, pp. 114-115)

Scientists are thus "obedient", "harnessed to the social mechanism" (*ibid.*, p. 145), "servants of authoritarian states" (*ibid.*, p. 196), victims of "alienation which in philosophical terminology is manifested as the separation of values and investigations, of knowledge and activity" (*ibid.*, p. 157). Similar quotes could easily be found in works by Habermas, Marcuse, Bloch, Adorno and others. Their formulations are poignant, but not their arguments.

The crux of the criticism of value-neutral science has remained entirely unclear. Why would the elimination of value-judgements from science in any way imply that scientists agree with what exists? It ought to be obvious to anyone that advocating value-neutrality means excluding *both* affirmative *and* negative attitudes to reality? The attempt to rid scientific standpoints of value-orientations represents simply another form of the fundamental aspiration of every escience — the aspiration for objectivity. Let us see how Albert Einstein described this tendency in science:

"The scientific way of thinking has a further characteristic. The concepts which it uses to build up its coherent systems do not express emotions. For the scientist, there is only 'being', but no wishing, no valuing, no good, no evil — in short, no goal. As long as we remain within the realm of science proper, we can never encounter a sentence of the type: 'Thou shalt not lie' . There is something like a Puritan's restraint in the scientist who seeks truth: he keeps away from everything voluntaristic or emotional. Incidentally, this trait is the result of a slow development, peculiar to modern Western thought." (Einstein 1953, p. 779)

If he wants to comprehend the truth about some aspect of reality, the scientist must try not to allow value-standpoints to influence him. They can only guide his comprehension in the wrong direction, in the direction of what he desires and approves, so that in the end he obtains a picture of his subject which does not correspond to reality. However, it clearly does not follow that because he proceeds in this way he is satisfied with present reality or opposed to change. With a strange persistence and without substantiation, the new Marxists accuse science and the value-neutral approach of coming to terms with what exists and advocating the *status quo*. It is strange to have to explain to philosophers such an elementary matter that value-neutral science is indeed not revolutionary, but *pari passu* it is not conservative either; it is value-neutral.

Neo-Marxists raise their voices against respect for facts, the cult of facts and "mere facticity". It is unclear, however, why an interest in facts should be censured. Actually the main task of science is to determine how things are in reality, to interpret the facts as objectively as possible and formulate laws describing them. Very often this kind of objective comprehension of "facticity" is what makes it possible to change those aspects of reality which are not in harmony with our values. If values are activated earlier, in the phase of investigation, they would in all probability hinder comprehension and prevent us from facing the truth and seeing things as they are.

The following deliberation is typical of neo-Marxists:

"So much the worse for facts! This is a maxim of verification which has, in given circumstances, resulted in so little adjustment to facts that it caused the English, American and French revolutions." (Bloch 1977a, p. 114)

Here we can clearly see how Bloch is confusing the epistemological and value status of facts, an elementary confusion typical of philosophers who follow "in Marx's footsteps". In fact, the slogan "So much the worse for facts" was never the maxim of verification for the English, American and French revolutionaries. It could possibly express their discontent with the situation in which they lived and their desire for radical social change. If they had really behaved in such a way as to not recognise the facts in the epistemological sense and not actually "adjusted" their actions "to the facts", their revolutions would simply have remained in their imagination.

At one point Horkheimer says:

"If we, however, look upon states of affairs given in perception as products which are in principle under human control, or should be, they lose the character of mere facticity." (Horkheimer 1968, p. 158)

Against whom is this invective about "mere facticity" directed? It would be interesting to see who Horkheimer and other neo-Marxists believe would be inclined to deny such a trivial truth as that "objects are in principle controlled by humans or at least should be". Those who zealously repeat and defend a platitude like this are fighting against windmills.

One of the main neo-Marxist objections to value-neutral science is that technology, its practical application, speaks only of the best way of implementing a goal, but offers no rational means of selecting it (Habermas 1971, p. 316, et. seq.). Science permits only technical rationality (determining the means when the goal has already been set) and leaves the sphere of goals and values entirely to irrationality. This "decisionism" and arbitrariness in selecting goals leads, it is said, to the alienation and spiritual disorientation of man today. A rational way of coping and orientating oneself should also be introduced into the sphere of values.

Neo-Marxists object to the value-neutrality of science because it permits *various* individual attitudes towards reality but does not commit itself to formulating and advocating the one attitude which, in their view, is the only rational one. The attitude of contemporary scientists who hold that, since there is no rational method for proving which values people should accept, such matters should be left to the sphere of individual choice, is totally unacceptable to them. This in no way makes personal orientations, desires and goal arbitrary or irrational, as Habermas, Horkheimer and Marcuse would have it, but rather makes them free.

Marx knows best

The humanist rhetoric of such thinkers on the subject of "authentic existence", "true happiness" and "disalienation" conceals authoritarianism and negates the autonomy of the personality. By claiming that someone other than people themselves knows better what their "genuine" interests are, contemporary Marxists are legitimising violence against the individual's fundamental freedoms. Two hundred years ago Kant warned about the dangerous consequences of violating the principle of autonomy even when justified "by benevolence towards people" or by the invocation of some "higher" goals:

> "A government established on the principle of benevolence towards the people, like the benevolence of a father toward his children, that is a *paternalistic government*, (*imperium paternale*) — where the subjects, like children under age who cannot distinguish what is genuinely useful or harmful to themselves, would be forced to behave purely passively, to rely only on the judgement of the head of state with regard to the question of how they *should* be happy, and to depend on his goodwill in wanting that at all — is the greatest *despotism* imaginable, a situation which abolishes all the freedom of the subjects and in which they therefore have no rights of any kind." (Kant 1914, p. 374)

Most scientists today believe that anyone advocating and arguing in favour of the realisation of certain social and political goals on the basis of alleged scientific principles and trying to underpin his proposals with the authority of his discipline, would be seriously exceeding his competence. This is what Max Weber says on the subject:

> "Those of our youth are in error who react to all by saying, 'Yes, but we happen to come to lectures in order to experience something more than mere analyses and statements of fact'. The error is that they seek in the professor something different from what stands before them. They crave a leader and not a teacher. But we are placed upon the platform solely as teachers. And these are two different things, as we can readily see." (Gerth & Mills 1948, p. 146)

New Marxists, of course, could not agree with such an attitude precisely because they are committed to just such a programme of teaching adults how they ought to behave. I will cite a few quotations from the works of contemporary Marxists, which clearly show that they present their philosophy as a collection of truths through which alone can individuals hope to discover their "true" values and aims:

"Genuine happiness presupposes comprehension of the truth: people knowing what is attainable for them as the highest possibility of their existence, what their genuine interest is." (Marcuse 1965, p. 150)

"In critical theory the concept of happiness has nothing in common with bourgeois conformism and relativism; it is part of the general, objective truth which holds good for all individuals, provided that in it the interests of all of them are abolished." (*ibid.*, p. 159)

"Those who have had the undeserved luck of not corresponding entirely in their spiritual make-up to prevailing norms .... must through moral effort and, so to speak, *instead of others* enunciate what the majority of those on whose behalf they speak cannot see, or forbid themselves to see, because of their adaptation to reality." (Adorno 1973, p. 51, italics added)

"What does it mean when we say 'a man knows his own interests best' — where does he get this knowledge from and where is the proof that his knowledge is right?" (Horkheimer 1974, p. 35)

"Philosophy is neither a tool nor a hard-and-fast rule. It can only herald the path of progress which is determined by logical and real necessities." (*ibid.*, p. 155)

"By relating consciousness to the whole of society, it becomes possible to infer the thoughts and feelings which men would have in a particular situation *if they were able to assess* both it and the interests arising from it .... Now class consciousness consists in fact of the appropriate and rational reactions 'imputed' to a particular position in the process of production. This consciousness is, therefore, neither the sum nor the average of what is thought or felt by the single individuals who make up the class." (Lukacs 1971, p. 51)

"This is precisely what gives the class struggle of the proletariat a special place amongst all class struggles: the fact that it acquires its sharpest weapon from *genuine science*, from *a clear insight into reality*. So long as the decisive aspects of class struggles in the past were ideologies of all kinds and religious, moral and other forms of 'distorted consciousness', the class struggle of the proletariat, the liberation war of the last subjugated class, found its battle cry and also its strongest weapon in the demonstration of the *undisguised truth*." (Lukacs 1977, p. 399, italics added)

Thus the goals we choose and set for ourselves should not be determined by our personal affinities and desires as individuals. Instead of this "purely subjective" and "arbitrary" factor, real values should be sought in the philosophical ideas offered by Marxism. These philosophical ideas are, unfortunately, not equally accessible to all, and certainly not

"in the way in which people with a similar intelligence quotient should be able to repeat natural sciences experiments or understand mathematical deductions." (Adorno 1973, p. 51)

Marxist philosophers are therefore called upon to decide, *on behalf of others*, what their genuine goals and interests are. Although others may have a "similar intelligence quotient", because of their "spiritual make-up" they are deprived of the philosophical dimension and so cannot penetrate to the "true science" and "clear insight into reality" which could show them what their "true happiness" is.

It is precisely here that the joint roots of Leninism and neo-Marxism are clearly discernible. What both of these standpoints have in common is the conviction that Marx's philosophy makes it possible to discover the "true" aims and interests of people although they themselves are not conscious of them. In *What Is To Be Done?*, Lenin put forward his fundamental idea that the working class, if left to its own devices, will develop a "trade union" and not an authentic class consciousness. Accordingly, the task of the minority instructed in Marxism is *to bring* to the workers *from without*, their "true" consciousness, even if this is entirely contrary to what they themselves might consider desirable and acceptable on the basis of their own *spontaneous* judgement. This standpoint contains the political quintessence of Bolshevism and it can help us the more readily to understand and explain many events in the history of Marxist-inspired movements. Thus when on 6th January 1918, Lenin and his Central Committee, forcible dissolved the legal constituent assembly, in which Social Revolutionaries had a large majority over the Bolsheviks, he was acting entirely in line with his own doctrine. He believed that his Marxist view of the world made him a better interpreter of the interests of the Soviet people than any democratically-held election or other expression of popular feeling![1] As the above questions show, many modern Marxists also claim on the basis of their philosophical insights that they are in a better position to judge what is in other people's "genuine" interests. From this follows the contention that the views of individuals should be ignored, as being "reified", "alienated" and the result of "false" aspirations. This declared disrespect for the autonomy of the individual implies the rejection of traditional democratic decision-making methods on political issues.

Pseudo-objectivism

From where do the neo-Marxist philosophers get the idea that they have the right to teach healthy adult persons what is good for them and what is not? This explicitly paternalistic attitude is shrouded in Hegelian terminology which is supposed to give it the appearance and dignity of a philosophical insight. For instance, in more recent Marxist literature it is claimed that people are not yet what they are (Adorno 1973, p. 274; Marcuse 1972, p. 111; Bloch 1977a, p. 195). This means that their empirical existence does not yet correspond to their real form of existence, that their "facticity" does not correspond to their concept, that they are alienated from their human essence. It is easy to perceive here the old distinction between facts and values, between "is" and "ought to". It cannot be erased or "overcome" by simply shrouding it with Hegelian and pseudo-objectivist terminology.

Like Hegel's alleged transcendence of Kant's dualism of the factual and the normative, the entire neo-Marxist activism is based on the exploitation of the ambiguity of such expressions as "true", "genuine", "real", "authentic", "what an object really is", "essence", "concept", etc. I will explain the crucial equivocation with a simple example. When we say that an object is *a true, genuine or real* diamond, we want to convey that its properties correspond to what our scientific knowledge tells us are the marks of a diamond. The expressions "true", "genuine" and "real" in this case indicate correspondence with a precise *theoretical* concept. Such expressions, however, have an entirely different function in other contexts. For example, when we say that some work gives us *true, genuine or real* satisfaction, we want to say that its properties put it at the top of the list of our personal preferences. The expressions "true", "genuine" and "real" in this context signify correspondence with certain *values*.

The claim that an object is a real diamond has a purely cognitive character because it simply describes the objective properties of the object concerned and has no value ingredients. On the other hand, to claim that some work gives us satisfaction is to express a value attitude — to make a statement of what we *subjectively* appreciate and consider desirable. The claim about the real diamond can be tested by entirely objective methods: what is at stake is whether the object has all the properties which satisfy the scientific criteria for something being a diamond. The claim about real satisfaction is impossible to test in this way because it is not a question of objective properties but of what different people consider to be real satisfaction. In short, science decides whether something is a real diamond, while individual value attitudes decide whether something affords real satisfaction.

By tirelessly exploiting the ambiguity of these expressions, neo-Marxists are able to present their own value attitudes as an objective philosophical comprehension of a higher order. They say that man is not yet what he *really* is, that he is alienated from his *true* essence, that he has not realised his *genuine* potential and so on. They are not aware that in ceasing to use explicit ethical terminology, they have not gone a single step further than Kant. The "is — ought" distinction cannot be transcended by adopting a quasi-objectivist Hegelian jargon in which certain value connotations are concealed and implicit. Neo-Marxists must decide in which of the *two* ways they want to interpret their muddled and ambiguous categories.

The *first* alternative is for them to understand "true human nature", "man's essence" and "genuine existence" as expressions relating to a way of life which certain theoretical research has determined as being generally characteristic of the human kind. In this case there is no reason whatsoever why we should want to manifest our "essential" properties or return to our true nature, if we have perhaps become "alienated" from it. What we discover about our "essence" in this sense need not necessarily be to our credit or appear to us as something for which we should strive. Suppose a radicalised sociobiology succeeded in proving that the essence of man's behaviour lies in his absolute selfishness (because selfishness is programmed by his genes); a humanist would then undoubtedly demand that man should become as alienated as possible from his own true essence!

The *other* method is to interpret the expressions "true", "genuine", "man's essence" as referring to a way of life which is in harmony with certain value attitudes and ideals. In this case the "return to human essence", "authentic existence" and "dis-alienation" would simply signify something of which neo-Marxists and people of similar ethical orientations approve and which they considered desirable. The reason they firmly reject such an interpretation is that they realise their philosophy would then be reduced to sheer moralising.

The Marxist "tendency"

There is no other method open to contemporary Marxists which would enable them to make their utopia desirable by means of philosophical arguments. Regardless of how profound the comprehensions of the young Marx's anthropology may be, his vision of the future cannot influence people's behaviour by telling them what man is, but only by telling them what *he ought to be*. It is understandable why Marxists are not prepared to accept either of the methods at their disposal. Without ethical connotations their philosophy ceases to be a call to action and remains in the sphere of pure theoretical knowledge; while with explicit ethical connotations it cannot be universalised because it may be rejected by anybody with *different* value attitudes. As is usually the case, a middle-of-the-road "dialectical" solution has to be found: a specious objectivist turn of phrase has been adopted which, due to its ambiguity and lack of precision, has allowed value qualifications to be almost imperceptibly drawn from it as the need arises. Without these expressions which contain a fundamental equivocation, the neo-Marxist standpoint would not only lose its force of persuasion, but could not even be formulated.

Crucial concepts such as "tendency" and "possibility" which are often used in contemporary Marxist literature have a similar status. For the sake of illustration, I will quote two passages from Bloch which demonstrate the way these concepts are used to provide a foundation for utopia:

".... we must differentiate very clearly between abstract utopias and those which become concrete ones. Social utopias in particular could have been abstract because their projection was not conveyed by the existing tendency or possibility ...." (Bloch 1977a, p. 95)

"It is no surprise therefore when Oscar Wilde says: 'A geographical map on which the country Utopia is not marked does not even deserve a glance.' From objects themselves there is a kind of line extended, true enough only by dots, towards something resembling that country, and no amount of erasing or concealment by all the positivists put together can divert it from what is actually going on. There are, therefore .... utopian edges not only of a being but also of the entire, already present existence and essence, which surround that which is present and actual with a much greater *objective-real possibility.*" (*ibid.*, p. 102)

If there really does exist a historical tendency which makes the achievement of Marxist utopia probable, it does not necessarily follow that we should therefore be satisfied, or that we should try to bring this process of achievement to an early conclusion. Historical tendencies can exist, and have existed, which should at all costs be kept within the sphere of unrealised possibilities. In connection with Bloch's concept of "objective-real possibilities", it can also be quite simply noted that even if it is an objectively real possibility for something to happen, this in itself does not mean that it is also a good thing for it to happen. Bloch and other Marxists are exploiting the other meaning of the concept of possibilities, which appears in sentences such as "he has realised all his possibilities" or "this young man has great possibilities", and which obviously refer *only* to possibilities of which the speaker approved. The expression "possibility", like the other expressions mentioned earlier, has all the advantages which make it convenient for the requirements of Marxist philosophy. It is essentially ambiguous, and the transition from its objective meaning to a meaning coloured by value is practically imperceptible. In this way the illusion is created that the desirability of Marxist utopia is proven by philosophical arguments.

Non-Marxists cannot criticise Marxism

Very often, and not without pride, neo-Marxists maintain that by their activist position they have achieved unity of theory and practice (for example, Lukacs 1977, p. 35 and p. 375; Bloch 1977b, p. 315; Lukacs 1967, p. 71 and pp. 126-127; Horkheimer 1968, pp. 179-180; Marcuse 1965, pp. 159-160). The contemplative attitude is "transcended" in Marxism by making activity and comprehension indivisible. Or, as Lukacs has said:

> "The essence of the proletarian class struggle can be determined by the fact that for it theory and practice coincide, that here comprehension leads to activity *without a transition*." (Lukacs 1977, p. 400 — italics are mine)

The direct consequence of such a fusion of the theoretical and the practical is that anybody whose activity is not in accordance with Marxism is simply demonstrating his inadequate comprehension. If indeed Marxist "comprehension leads without transition to activity" then by contraposition we can conclude that an activity which is not Marxist entails lack of Marxist comprehension. As many critics have noted (Kolakowski 1978, III, p. 298; Tucker 1972, p. 229; Acton 1955, p. 177), the alleged unity of theory and practice is in fact a mystification which *a priori* prevents any kind of rational critique of Marxist doctrine.

It is beyond dispute that we can criticise only that which we understand. If we accept (on the basis of this "fusion" of the theoretical and practical) that Marxist philosophy is really *only* understood by people who act in keeping with it (that is, who accept it), it follows that this philosophy can only be criticised by those who agree with it! It is difficult to imagine a more agreeable theoretical position than one which rejects *a limine* any objection by falling back on the universal explanation that he who questions the "vanguard doctrine" is merely proving he has not understood it. Acton's conclusion seems to me, therefore, entirely appropriate:

> "In this way the Marxist is enabled to argue that no-one who does not work on behalf of the Marxist Communist Parties can really understand what Marxism is. Once more the similar-

53

ity with Pascal's advice — to learn to be a Christian by going to Mass — is obvious."

ABSTRACTNESS

The basic characteristic of the Marxist utopia is its extreme abstractness and indeterminacy. While Bloch and other Marxists have made great efforts to convince us that their vision of the future is very concrete, their assurances are in vain as long as they do not set out the details and specific aspects of their utopia. To use an analogy by Ayer (1963, p. 277) from a different context: just as one cannot prove that horses have wings by arbitrarily using the word "horse" to mean what is ordinarily meant by "sparrow", in the same vein one cannot prove that Marxian utopia is concrete by using the word "concrete" to denote things without any specific characteristics.

What kind of utopia?

Unlike Marxists, the utopian socialists have described their ideals for a social system in great detail and in vivid colours. Indeed, that is one of the reasons why none of these utopias offers us a political model. Many of the details they have proposed with great enthusiasm would not be considered desirable by the majority of people. They also include ideas which should evoke general revulsion. Thus, for example, in Cabet's *Icaria*, the freedom of the press is severely restricted. In Bacon's *New Atlantis*, the presentation of any work of nature in a decorative and artificial manner and not just as it is, is banned under the threat of payment of a fine and disgrace. In More's *Utopia*, repeated adultery is punishable by death and in Campanella's *Civitas Solis* "any woman who puts rouge on her face out of a desire to be more beautiful, or wears shoes with high heels to look taller or dresses with trains to hide her ugly legs, would be punished by death." (Campanella 1941, p. 134)

But even if we disregard these and similar details, the fact remains that historical utopias can no longer arouse any serious interest today. They are the product of a time when it was believed that a certain fundamental and global change in the social system could bring about general happiness and be equally acceptable to all. Their concrete and evolved visions of the future are unacceptable to us, not only because they are historically obsolete and because the authors' ideals were different from ours, but for a much deeper reason inherent in the very idea of utopia. Thus we must accept the fact that people are fundamentally different from one another and with regard to the form of a future society they cherish desires, aspirations and interests which regularly clash. Since experience teaches us that proposals for piecemeal political reforms give rise to sharp disputes and disagreements, how much *naivete* is needed to believe that everybody without exception would welcome or accept a fundamental, global change in the social system!

The Marxist utopia has retained a certain topical appeal due largely to its abstract nature. Marxists usually describe their vision of the future with words coloured by values which are so general and so undefined that they are acceptable to most people. At the same time they carefully avoid indicating the specific attributes and qualities of this "Kingdom of Freedom" which might be the source of objections from people with different value judgements. This creates the illusion that a completely new form of society has been discovered which, unlike others before it, is ideal because it brings general justice and universal happiness.

For the sake of illustration I will mention just a few of the most frequent ways neo-Marxists describe their utopia: "a community of free people", "a sensible society", "the transformation of the social entity", "an association of free people in which everyone has an equal opportunity for development", "a just society", "the transcendence of social injustice", "a dignified, peaceful and happy future for society", "a total historical act", "the creation of a genuine human community", "an authentic existence", "a radical change in man", "the realisation of man's possibilities", etc.

It is quite clear that hardly anyone today is against "man realising his possibilities", or against "a community of free people" or "a just society". If Marxism remains at the level of such abstract and undefined phrases it really does become almost generally acceptable, but for this very reason it is in danger of losing all its meaning and becoming trivial and uninteresting. I think that in this respect the brief dialogue which Proudhon had with the judge at his trial in 1848 should be instructive for contemporary Marxists. The judge asked him whether he was a socialist.

"Certainly."

"Well, but what, then, is Socialism?"

"It is," replied Proudhon, "every aspiration towards the improvement of society."

"But in that case," very justly remarked the magistrate, "we are all socialists."

"That is precisely what I think," rejoined Proudhon.

(Quoted: in Draper 1977, p. 98)

Proudhon was, of course, wrong; not all people in his time were socialists. Similarly, not everybody today is a Marxist, though most people would have no objection to many of the general aspirations found in abstract Marxist phrases with positive value connotations.

The terms which Marxists use to describe their utopia are in fact parasitic or "supervenient" predicates. They do not describe social phenomena directly, but are true of such phenomena only by virtue of the fact that these phenomena possess some other properties which we may call their "primary properties". For instance: a society is just (supervenient property) by virtue of the fact that relations in it are regulated in a certain way (primary property); a community is an association of free people (super-venient property) by virtue of the fact that the life of its members has certain quite concrete and specific features (primary property). And so on.

A society can possess abstract and value-coloured properties (supervenient properties) only if it first possesses certain value-neutral properties which define its structure and method of organ-isation. In talking about their utopia, Marxists have failed to do the one thing without which the entire story they tell makes no sense at all: they have not begun to describe what this ideal society of theirs looks like, that is, they have not described its primary properties, only its supervenient ones.

Let us imagine that someone demands that houses should be built which are more stable, last longer and are more comfortable and cheaper than today's houses. Stability, durability, comfort and low prices, however, are supervenient properties: a house can have them only by virtue of it having definite primary properties (the method of construction, the material from which it is built, etc). It should be obvious, therefore, that making such a demand is not the same as providing a blueprint for the construction of such houses. The demand merely sets out the supervenient properties, the desirable features to be achieved by the proposed design. It does not begin to specify the primary properties which the design must incorporate in order to achieve those objectives.

In exactly the same way, despite repeated claims to the con-trary, Marxists have completely failed to provide us with a blue-print for a new type of society. They have simply enumerated the obviously desirable objectives which, it is hoped, will supervene on the primary properties specified in such a blueprint, if and when the blueprint is prepared and the plan is finally executed. Just as houses cannot be built from stability, durability and comfort, but only from bricks, cement, wood and other building materials placed in a definite structural relation to one another, so more perfect forms of society cannot be constructed from such objec-tives as "just", "humane" and "wise", but only by an actual re-organisation of social relations (for example, by fundamental change in the electoral system, an increase in citizens' legal security, more efficient public control of the activity of the politicians, etc).

Marx tells us very little when he says in his "Contribution to the Critique of Hegel's Philosophy of Right: Introduction" that "all the conditions in which a man is an abased, enslaved, abandoned, contemptible being, should be overthrown." (Tucker 1978, p. 60) We probably all agree that relations which "abase" and "enslave" human beings should be abolished, but key differences in political judgement arise precisely over *which* kind of relations should be considered responsible for this state of affairs. It is precisely in reply to the question *what* should be changed and *how* should it change to create "a more just" and "humane" society, that people today will give totally different answers. Everyone can agree on the ends. But to expect similar unanimity concerning the means by which those ends are to be achieved, is like asking for the moon and expecting to receive it.

The picture of Marxian utopia sometimes appears to be a generally acceptable ideal simply because it does not contain any specific programme for changing society, which would be much more and, for the Marxist taste, much too controversial. This utopia has only abstract qualities, with positive value connotations which do not tell us at all what this "just society" would really look like. That alone is why it was possible for the Marxian vision of the future not to be compromised by various unsuccessful attempts at forming a society on the basis of Marx's political philosophy. It has always been possible to say that these failed attempts at constructing a socialist utopia were merely "deviations" and "distortions" of his "true" ideas which should continue to represent a model. If, however, a political programme only amounts to a call to strive towards a "just", "humane" and "free" society, then that programme can never be compromised, not because it offers the best solution to all human misfortunes and problems, but simply because it consists of empty abstractions and high-sounding meaningless phrases.

Vagueness licenses opportunism

It would, however, be wrong to conclude that, because of its vagueness, Marxist political philosophy contains nothing controversial. On the contrary, since it was believed that Marx's vision of the future, transcendental and sacred, gave meaning to all of human "prehistory", the view emerged that it was permissible to use every possible means in order to achieve this "goal above all goals". Political action also began to be evaluated increasingly on the basis of whether society was "objectively" getting nearer to this distant ideal, while evaluations of such action in terms of ordinary moral considerations were increasingly pushed into the background. Finally, and quite consistently, a decisive role was given to the principle of tactical efficacy and opportunism, according to which *no* action (not even the most morally repulsive) is to be rejected *a priori* if it seems the best way to achieve the desired end. By thus abolishing the validity of ethical principles and moral considerations in politics, Marxism has opened up to its followers wide scope for tactical moves and an unusual amount of practical flexibility. As we have seen, this derives from a rigid and unreserved commitment to the idea of the revolutionary transformation of society. As Lukacs so aptly put it: "*.... the non-rigidity of communist tactics is the direct consequence of the rigidity of communist principles.*" (Lukacs 1972, p. 54)

Those who proclaim and try to realise the idea of changing society in the spirit of Marxism are not bound by their "programme" precisely because its abstractness provides no hint about how to act in particular political situations. The invocation of Marxian utopia has legitimised the slogan "land to the peasants" and, a little later, the taking away of land and collectivisation. It has given licence to the slogan "all power to the soviets" and, a little earlier, opposition to the institution of soviets. It has justified opposition to a one-party system and, in another period of history, the introduction of such a system.[2] What this illustrates is the well-established fact that those who tie themselves to a political programme full of grand words but lacking in specific content, have completely free hand in pursuit of their objectives. This is also the source of the principle of extreme political pragmatism which expressly characterises Marxist historical practice and was clearly and concisely formulated by Lenin:

"In politics there is only one principle and one truth: what profits my opponent hurts me and *vice versa*." (Quoted in Ulam 1966, p. 226)

Moreover the fact that the Marxian utopia was abstract and without content, not only allowed its champions unrestricted freedom of action, but also made it possible for them to preserve the illusion that they were realising a certain political programme when all they were doing was trying to stay in power at any cost in all kinds of situations.

Criticism is not prescription

At times, it seems as though Marxists believe that positive and specific directions for achieving their utopia will arise out of their merciless criticism of modern society. This expectation, however, proves in the event to be unfounded. No doubt much of the Marxist criticism of the consumer society, of the negative effect of technology and of the modern way of life in general is justified and uncontroversial; but it does not follow that it is possible to discern a remedy to such social ills simply by drawing attention to them.

No-one denies, for instance, that the large number of traffic accidents and casualties is an extremely undesirable feature of present-day life. But despite general agreement, for the time being we simply cannot see a way of eliminating this deplorable situation without at the same time depriving ourselves of the benefits of short and comfortable journeys and a great saving in time and effort.

Similarly, although we can perhaps accept some aspects of the Marxist critique of contemporary society, we are not thereby committed to the abolition of these "negative" phenomena by the overthrow of whole society in which they occur. They may be a necessary price we have to pay for some other advantages of contemporary life to which we attach considerable value and which we would not want to do without. Science and technology are frequently the target of attacks by neo-Marxists, but although they are presumably not in favour of going back to what the Americans call "the horse and buggy days" before the explosion of modern scientific technology, their works offer no guidance on how the "negative" aspects of these modern achievements can be eliminated whilst preserving all that is "positive" like advances in medical science, electrical and electronic equipment in the home, rapid and efficient methods of travel, communication and information processing, and the rest.

To be realistic the rational man should, so it seems to me, reconcile himself to the fact that any kind of society which may evolve or be constructed artificially will have its good and bad aspects and that there is no way of achieving paradise on earth. Consequently, even if we accept the Marxists' objections to some features of contemporary society, it does not follow that we, or any one else, knows how to change things for the better.

It is well known that radical programmes for the transformation of society have often been based purely on dissatisfaction with the existing state of affairs, and have not contained detailed and precise proposals about the form the new method of social organisation should take. This is also the main reason why many of them have led to a situation far worse than that existing before any changes were made. If there is no projection of the future which can be compared with the situation as it exists and thereby facilitate a rational choice, there is no reason to expect that a change, motivated merely by dissatisfaction, will be more acceptable than the *status quo*.

It is most instructive in this context to examine the standpoint of a typical radical thinker such as Auguste Blanqui. He ridiculed those socialists who devoted too much time to speculating about the form of a future society and said they reminded him of people standing on the bank of a river discussing what lies on the other side. "Let us cross over and see!" Blanqui proposes. It is not clear, however, why he was so sure that on crossing over to the other side he would not regret having done so and seek, if at all possible, to return quickly to his more cautious comrades.

Guidance on changes in the direction of society cannot, therefore, be derived simply from criticism (however philosophical!) of the existing situation. It can only come from a detailed and well-substantiated programme of transformation which the majority of individual members of the society in question will accept as the best solution and vote for in a democratic manner. It should, therefore, be concluded that the philosophers' stone for which Marxists have been stubbornly searching to transmute our imperfect society into the "Kingdom of Freedom" does not exist. What should make us wonder in particular is their belief that this can be achieved by attentively studying what was written in quite different times by a young man 140 years ago.

IV. IN PLACE OF GOD?

My earlier analysis of the foundations of scientific socialism and the examination of neo-Marxism in the second part of this essay lead to the conclusion that both main attempts at providing a foundation for the Marxian vision of the future have proved unsuccessful. Marxian utopia rests on sand. This conclusion should not be seen as unexpected because Marxism was conceived from the beginning in such a way as to make its claims necessarily unrealistic and in principle unrealisable. It was entirely illusory and mistaken to try to legitimise the programme for a radical and fundamental change in society either by scientific or by philosophical arguments. The implementation of a political programme cannot be justified by its alleged foundation on some epochal scientific or philosophical discoveries, but only and exclusively by its being in line with the value judgements of individuals whose full autonomy is acknowledged.

No matter how strong the scientific or philosophical arguments in favour of any utopia, it must nevertheless in the end be judged by individuals who, on the basis of their *subjective* value assessments, will decide whether this radical change is acceptable to them. An *objective* perception of an ideal form of society could, therefore, be said to be *a contradictio in adiecto*.

Many people, however, can still not abandon the unyielding desire to find an objective and generally valid method by which the "right" way of life for man and the "right" method of organising society can be established as a matter of scientific or philosophical demonstration. They cannot reconcile themselves to the idea that human values can be said to be "arbitrary" and "irrational", that is, that they are a matter for the individual consciousness and cannot be justified by or founded on anything else. Although these arguments are, as we have seen, invalid and fundamentally mistaken, the Marxist standpoint still has a considerable following.

How are we to explain the fact that Marxism has been relatively widely accepted amongst contemporary thinkers, despite the fact that this philosophy is not exactly renowned for the rationality of its foundations? One answer which deserves our attention, is contained in Czeslaw Milosz's claim that the success of the Marxian utopia is "mainly due to the intellectuals' desire to have their values guaranteed, if not by God, at least by history".

FOOTNOTES

1. It is often overlooked that the Bolsheviks themselves at first recognised the legality of the constituent assembly, as is clearly shown by the fact that elections were held *after* they came to power. Their subsequent opposition was caused simply by the final result with which the leaders of the October Revolution could not reconcile themselves and which they apparently had not expected: three quarters of the population voted against their policies! The painful impression made by the dissolution of the representational body is attested to by Maxim Gorky who said at the time:
   "The best among the Russian people have for almost a hundred years lived for the idea of a constituent assembly — a political forum where the entire Russian democracy could freely express its will. For this idea thousands of intellectuals, tens of thousands of workers and peasants have perished in prisons, in exile and at hard labour, or died on the gallows or under the bullets of the firing squads. Rivers of blood have flowed as a sacrifice to this sacred idea — yet now, the 'people's commissars' gave the order to shoot down the crowd demonstrating in honor of this idea ..." (Abramovich 1962, p. 128)

2. Such sudden reversals and conspicuous inconsistencies of the policy are nearly always described in Marxist writings as "stages" of the historical development.

WORKS CITED

Abramovitch, R.R. 1962: *The Soviet Revolution*. London: George Allen & Unwin.
Acton, H.B. 1965: *The Illusion of the Epoch*. London: Routledge & Kegan Paul.

Adorno, T. 1973: *Negative Dialektik* (*Gesammelte Schriften*, Band 6). Frankfurt am Main: Suhrkamp Verlag.

Aron, R. 1967: *Les Etapes de la pensee sociologique*. Paris: Gallimard.

Ayer, A.J. 1963: *Philosophical Essays*. New York: Macmillan.

Becker, J.F. 1977: *Marxian Political Economy*. Cambridge: Cambridge University Press.

Blanshard, B. 1966: "Reflections on Economic Determinism"; *Journal of Philosophy*, 63, 169-178.

Blaug, M. 1976: "Kuhn versus Lakatos or Paradigms versus Research Programmes in the History of Economics", in: S.J. Latsis (ed.) *Method and Appraisal in Economics*. Cambridge: Cambridge University Press.

Bloch, E. 1977a: *Tuebinger Einleitung in die Philosophie*. Frankfurt am Main: Suhrkamp Verlag.

" 1977b: *Das Prinzip Hoffnung* (Kapitel 1-32). Frankfurt am Main: Suhrkamp Verlag.

Boehm-Bawerk, E. 1921: *Geschichte und Kritik der Kapitalzins-Theorien*. Jena: Gustav Fischer.

" 1975: *Karl Marx and the Close of His System*. London: Merlin Press.

Bose, A. 1975: *Marxian and Post-Marxian Political Economy*. Harmondsworth: Penguin.

Campanella, T. 1941: *La Citta del Sole* (testo italiano e testo latino — a cura di Norberto Bobbio). Torino: Giulio Einaudi.

Camus, A. 1951: *L'Homme revolte*. Paris: Gallimard.

Cohen, G.A. 1979: "The Labour Theory of Value and the Concept of Exploitation": *Philosophy and Public Affairs*, 8, 338-360.

Cole, G.D.H. 1961: *Marxism and Anarchism* (A History of Socialist Thought, Vol. II). London: Macmillan.

Draper, H. 1977: *Karl Marx's Theory of Revolution*. New York & London: Monthly Review Press.

Durkheim, E. 1928: *Le Socialisme*. Paris: Felix Alcan.

Einstein, A. 1953: "The Laws of Science and the Laws of Ethics"; in: H. Feigl & M. Brodbeck (eds.), *Readings in the Philosophy of Science*. New York: Appleton-Century-Crofts.

Engels, F. undated: *Development of Socialism from Utopia to Science*. Edinburgh: Socialist Labour Press.

Gellner, E. 1974: *The Devil in Modern Philosophy*. London: Routledge & Kegan Paul.

Gerth, H.H. & C. Wright Mills (eds.) 1948: *From Max Weber: Readings in Sociology*. London: Routledge & Kegan Paul.

Habermas, J. 1971: *Theorie und Praxis*. Frankfurt am Main: Suhrkamp Verlag.

Hilferding, R. 1949: *Boehm-Bawerk's Criticism of Marx*. London: Merlin Press.

Horkheimer, M. 1974: *Zur Kritik der instrumentellen Vernunft*. Frankfurt am Main: Athenaeum Fischer Taschenbuch Verlag.

1968: *Kritische Theorie*. II Frankfurt am Main: S. Fischer Verlag.

Howard, M.C. & King, J.C. 1975: *The Political Economy of Marx*. London: Longman.

Kant, I. 1914: "Ueber den Gemeinspruch: Das mag in der Theorie richtig sein, taugt aber nicht fuer die Praxis", in: I. Kant: *Werke*, VI. Berlin: B. Cassirer.

Kolakowski, L. 1978: *Main Currents of Marxism*. Oxford: Oxford University Press.

Lange, O. 1970: "Marxian Economics and Modern Economic Theory"; in: M. Curtis (ed.), *Marxism*. New York: Atherton Press.

Lenin, V.I. 1953: *What Is To Be Done?* Selected Works, Vol.I, Part I. London: Lawrence and Wishart.

Lukacs, G. 1967: *Lenin*. Neuwied & Berlin: Luchterhand.
"   1971: *History and Class Consciousness*. London: Merlin Press.
"   1972: *Tactics and Ethics (Political Writings 1919-1929)*. London: NLB.
"   1977: *Geschichte und Klassenbewusstsein*. Darmstadt & Neuwied: Luchterhand.
Marcuse, H. 1965: *Kultur und Gesellschaft*. I. Frankfurt am Main: Suhrkamp Verlag.
"   1972: *One Dimensional Man*. London: Abacus.
Marx, K. 1935: *Value, Price and Profit*. New York: International Publishers.
"   1962: "Erster Entwurf zum *Buergerkrieg in Frankreich*. In: K. Marx & F. Engels, *Werke* 17. Berlin: Dietz Verlag.
"   1968: *Theorien ueber, den Mehrwert*. III; in:K. Marx & F. Engels, *Werke* 26.3. Berlin: Dietz Verlag.
"   1982: *Capital*, Vol. 1-3. London: The Pelican Marx Library.
McLellan, D. 1973: *Karl Marx*. London: Macmillan.
Meek, R. 1967: *Economics and Ideology and Other Essays*. London: Chapman & Hall
"   1977: *Smith, Marx & After*. London: Chapman & Hall.
Morishima, M.1973: *Marx's Economics.* Cambridge: Cambridge University Press
Napoleoni, C. 1974: *Ricardo und Marx*. Frankfurt am Main: Suhrkamp Verlag.
Nozick, R. 1964: *Anarchy, State and Utopia*. Oxford: Basil Blackwell.
Popper, K. R. 1959: *Logic of Scientific Discovery*. London: Hutchinson.
Robinson, J. 1964: *Economic Philosophy*. Harmondsworth: Penguin.
"   1965: "Marxism: Religion and Science"; in: *Collected Economic Papers*, III, Oxford: Blackwell.
"   1966: *An Essay on Marxian Economics*. London: Macmillan.
Roemer, J.E. 1982: *A General Theory of Exploitation and Class*. Cambridge, Mass.: Harvard University Press.
Rubin, I.I. 1978: *Ogledi o Marksovoj teoriji vrijednosti*. Zagreb: "Stvarnost".
Samuelson, P.A. 1966: "Economics and the History of Ideas"; in: *The Collected Scientific Papers*, II, Cambridge, Mass.: The M.I.T. Press.
"   1971: "Understanding the Marxian Notion of Exploitation", *The Journal of Economic Literature*, 9, 399-431.
Schumpeter, J.A. 1954: *History of Economic Analysis*. New York: Oxford University Press.
Sombart, W. 1908: *Sozialismus und Soziale Bewegung*. Jena: Verlag von Gustav Fischer.
Spiegel, H.W. 1952: *The Development of Economic Thought*. New York: John Wiley & Sons.
Steedman, I. 1977: *Marx After Sraffa*. London: NLB.
Sweezy, P.M. 1946: *The Theory of Capitalist Development*. London: Dennis Dobson Limited.
Sik, O. 1972: *Der dritte Weg*. Hamburg: Hoffman und Campe.
Tucker, R.C. 1972: *Philosophy and Myth in Karl Marx*. Cambridge: Cambridge University Press.
"   1978: *The Marx-Engels Reader*. New York: W.W. Norton & Company, Inc.
Ulam, A. 1966: *Lenin and the Bolsheviks*. London: Secker & Warburg.
Wolfe, B. 1967: *Marxism, One Hundred Years in the Life of a Doctrine*. London: Chapman & Hall.

☆

Part II
An armed prophesy

FROM THEORETICAL TO HISTORICAL CRITIQUE

Domenico Settembrini

Biographical note

DOMENICO SETTEMBRINI was born in 1929 at Cupramontana in the Italian region of Marche. He is now full professor of history of political doctrines at the University of Pisa, where he had previously taught the history of workers' movement and trade-unionism and where he had also graduated. Some of his works are mentioned in the bibliography at the end of his paper, others include the following books in Italian: *Socialism and Revolution after Marx*, Guida, Naples, 1974, and *Fascism — the Imperfect Counter-Revolution*, Sansoni, Florence, 1978. He writes for *La Nazione* of Florence and *Il Resto del Carlino* of Bologna. In English he has published: "Mussolini and the Legacy of Revolutionary Socialism" in *Journal of Contemporary History*, reprinted in G. Mosse ed., *International Fascism*, Saga Publications, 1979: "Lenin and Mussolini" in G. Urban ed., *Eurocommunism*, Temple-Smith, London, 1978; and "Capitalism, Socialism and the State" in *Survey*, Autumn 1980.

Initially Domenico Settembrini taught at secondary schools and was a political militant, having been a member of the Italian Communist Party 1953-1958. In the mid-1970s, his works began the radical criticism of the Marxian ideology which up till then had been dominant in Italy and hardly discussed at all.

The essay by Sesardic is clear, exhaustive and unexceptionable in showing the theoretical and scientific inconsistency of Marxism. But he gives only an indirect and partial reply to the question he poses of why Marxism has been so successful, while so many other versions of utopian socialism have been "practically forgotten". Sesardic states that the purpose of his essay is precisely to inquire whether this contrast is the result of "a really fundamental difference between the two types of socialist doctrine'" or whether it is due to "some particular reason". He explicitly rejects the former hypothesis. Despite Marx's claim that his scientific apparatus erected an insurmountable barrier between his own socialism and the socialism of his rivals, Sesardic concludes that Marx's doctrine is also utopian and not substantially different from those of "utopian socialists". The reader of the essay is left with the impression that the success of the one and the failure of the others is due "to some particular reason", entirely accidental of which the essay says nothing.

This does not mean that the theoretical critique of the scientific basis of Marxism is irrelevant for the historic comprehension of the fate of the movement. On the contrary, it is its indispensable premise. Clearly as long as we look at the world through Marx's spectacles, what has happened to Marxism in opposition to the forecasts must remain incomprehensible in principle, because it should not have happened at all if the doctrine had fulfilled its claim to unearth the iron laws of historical developments.

In other words, if Sesardic, taking advantage of a century of scholarly critique, had not made it clear that Marxism is myth rather than science, it would be as impossible to interpret its metamorphoses as it has always been to write, under rigorous scientific criteria, a history of any religion so long as the uniqueness and divine origin of its scriptural revelation had enjoyed an uncontested authority in the conscience of the scholars. An idea claiming to be absolutely true and absolutely just — whether it is the word of Christ, or of Mohammed, or of Marx — should not strictly speaking be subject to change or transformation of its content. By definition, there is a history only of those things which are exclusively human and hence imperfect, relative, changeable, transitional.

The theoretical critique, by shedding light on the utopian nature of Marx's doctrine, not only represents a methodologically necessary condition to proceed to the historical critique, but supplies this latter with a least two results. It explains why the victory of the movement did not correspond to the eschatological-messianic expectations of the mass of the most simple-minded followers — men can yearn for the absolute but can never reach it. It also explains why the assumption of power has come about in countries and at times at variance with what the letter of the doctrine anticipated, that is outside the countries of most advanced capitalism — and how the opposite could happen, given that *Das Kapital* is not a science but wishful thinking. What, however, theoretical criticism of a rational type cannot explain by itself is why, amongst utopias, the Marxist utopia could impose itself on reality, albeit at the price of many metamorphoses, when all other utopias disintegrated and vanished from collective memory.

Why did Marxism succeed?

Since the development was exactly the opposite of what Marx predicted — not towards ever greater immiserization of working classes but towards their rising welfare; not towards proletarization of middle classes but towards their growing articulation and expansion — it might be thought that the best resolution of the problem was to attribute the success obtained in the backward Russia of 1917 to "some particular reason", entirely extraneous to the ideological armoury of Marxism.

Certainly, it could not be denied that in the achievements of Marxism — as in any other human event — chance has played an important, even decisive role. If circumstances had not allowed Lenin to conquer power in a lucky strike, there would not have been revolution in the name of Marx and the idea might have remained safely in the books. On the other hand, it is true that in the circumstances the content of Marx's idea, its genetic code, must have been particularly appropriate, or it could not have profited from this opportunity to the extent it did.

Here we touch on the problem Marxism poses for an historian of ideas. Taken literally, Marxism put itself forward as a revolutionary project to follow the triumph of capitalism and overcome national barriers. The revolution is foreseen as an insurrection of the proletariat against international bourgeoisie in the West. Elsewhere the order of the day would remain the arrival of national capitalism on the ruins of various sorts of feudalism. In reality, Marxism is victorious only where it succeeds to channel in its own direction the endeavours for industrial development and for national pre-eminence. Theoretical Marxism is a post-capitalist and internationalist socialism, but Marxism once put into practice turns out to be a socialism of the national-populist kind. However important external circumstances they cannot entirely explain this extraordinary metamorphosis. What has to be done is to identify the latent germs of national populism, without which Marxism would not have been capable of adapting so efficiently to the circumstances, by turning necessity into virtue.

Looking at things from this point of view, we notice that inconsistencies and theoretical defects of Marxism can be very valuable. Let us take, for example, the strategy of the progressive watering down of theorems, which Sesardic shows Marxists indulge in systematically to avoid being disproved by events. Although this strategy can only be deplored by a scholar, it is indispensable for founders and apostles of any faith that wishes in Marx's words "to transform the world". It is especially indispensable for those of a faith such as Marxism which claims to be based on science and which, therefore, could not survive being shown wrong when confronted with facts.

For Marxism to profit from the circumstances prevailing in Russia in 1917, the main prerequisite was to have preserved the capacity of inflaming the hearts of popular masses. This would not have happened if Kautsky, confronted with the crisis triggered off by Bernstein, had not reacted by watering down the theoretical content of Marxism. The most significant example of this manoeuvre was Kautsky's modification, from the rising of absolute immiserization to the rising of the relative immiserization. It is not a coincidence that his contemporaries gave Kautsky the name of "the red pope"[1], while communist historians later recognised his merit of having kept alive the "memory of revolution at a non-revolutionary time"[2] and so of having contributed to the later establishment of Leninism in Europe where it could not otherwise have taken root.

Marxist "duplicity"

This manoeuvre is obviously a "merit" which becomes a grave demerit in the eyes of those who reject revolutionary mysticism and note that in Italy and in Germany, where infatuation with Lenin and the Russian revolution was at its height; this move has served only to weaken democracy and contribute to its downfall. But the fact remains that Marxism always moved on two planes: one theoretical-fideistic, the other political-pragmatic.. The first is the plane of absolute certainty, of a providential concept of history, conceived as a process destined to end in communism of limitless abundance, a society without any more economic problems, without classes and without government, after having passed through a well-determined sequence of stages — slavery, feudalism, capitalism. The other is the plane of continuously changing strategies, inspired by changing circumstances and learning from past experiences, with the purpose of gaining total power. This power (viz. the dictatorship of the proletariat) is, in turn, considered to be the indispensable instrument required to validate the theory by forcing the overflowing social reality to run within pre-ordained schemes.

This fundamental "duplicity" of theory and practice is sufficient evidence that Marxists themselves are the first not to believe without reservations in Marx's forecasts which are supposedly scientific. If anybody really believes that the locomotive of history is running along a track which inevitably leads to exactly the same destination which he is longing for, it makes no sense for him to want to take control of the levers so as to be able to make the locomotive change direction even at the risk of derailing it. The people who are tempted to violate reality or to "play tricks with history" — as Trotsky put it in a polemic with Lenin — are those who are afraid, perhaps unconsciously, that reality and history are moving along a course different from what they want them to take.

Usually it is thought that Marx derived his revolutionary imperative from theory. According to the theory, capitalism is destined by its very nature to become a brake on technical development after having been its stimulus. After having launched the movement towards automation, capitalism would become an insurmountable hindrance to its advent. As a result, the revolution which subjectively is the only alternative for the working class to an ever worsening immiserization, objectively destroys capitalism and thus becomes a necessary route for completing the emancipation of man from nature. In the formation of his thought, however, Marx first postulated the revolutionary imperative which he deduced from purely philosophical-religious premises, and only afterwards elaborated his economic theory to underpin the revolution with an entirely mundane and rational justification of a materialist-productivist type — to unblock the way towards automation.

In other words, Marx's revolution is not indicated by economic diagnosis as the only remedy capable of restarting the productive apparatus blocked by capitalists. Rather it is exactly the other way round: Marx arbitrarily puts together a diagnosis because he wants to persuade himself and others that the revolution is not a "voluntaristic" and subjective aspiration but a rational and necessary objective.

In psychoanalytical terms, what is involved is a "rationalisation". In economic terms, Marx produces out of the blue from his mental laboratory an entirely imaginary capitalism which behaves as required to justify and keep up revolutionary hopes. The pertinacity with which Marx writes *Das Kapital*, a boundless and unfinished work, is due to his suspicion, if not awareness, that the real capitalism was behaving in a way contrary to his expectations.

The French Marxist scholar, Henri Lefebvre, has recently admitted that "in modern countries such as United States or Northern Europe. . . exactly that has happened which Marx judged impossible." Trying to explain how this can come about, Lefebvre finally asks whether there could be "somewhere in Marx a fault, an error which is reflected in the total edifice".[3] To this question, another Marxist, Paul Sweezy, replies that Marx and Engels saw that social developments were progressively moving away from what they expected, but

> "did not know how to insert in their teaching the inevitable conclusion that the working classes of the centre. . . had been transformed into a reforming force which was trying to improve their members' situation within the structure of the capitalist system."[4]

Keeping up revolutionary faith

In reality, Marx and Engels were fully aware of what was happening in England. Their correspondence included frequent lamentations, especially by Engels, about the lack of ardour in the English working class which was becoming *bourgeois* under the influence of high wages. But bringing this awareness into the theory would have meant surrendering to reformist tendencies and giving them scientific approval. To avoid this, Marx used the typically Hegelian expedient of juxtaposing an essence of capitalism, constructed *ad hoc* to give it an unequivocally revolutionary meaning, to its superficial appearance with unequivocally reformist features. It is an Hegelian axiom that the contrast between the essential and the empirical will in the end be resolved by the triumph of the former over the latter. It follows that the purpose of Marx's theory was not to analyse our experience so as to forecast as precisely as possible the most probable future course of the economy, but to shelter the conscience of revolutionaries from reformist temptations by reassurances that eventually the conditions for a victorious revolution must prevail, regardless of all appearances and experience to the contrary.

Das Kapital was not written as a scientific treatise but as a book of faith. The faith, however, was not proclaimed to console but to provoke by any means, however different from what was explicitly stated, the violent overthrow of the capitalist-liberal system. That was the motivation behind the whole theoretical reasoning of Marx.

During the years between 1843 and 1850 — when he anticipated in the *Communist Manifesto* and *Wage Labour and Capital* the substance of *Das Kapital* — Marx experimented with approaches which would finally come together in Lenin's synthesis: tha national-populist and anarchic-jacobin. On the one hand, he theorized that the communist revolution should simultaneously involve Europe and North America and be led by England, then the most advanced capitalist country. At the same time, he did not conceal that he wanted more than anything else to push backward Germany into a leading position. With this in mind, on 1st January, 1849, Marx called for a revolutionary war of European countries against England. By March 1850, Marx was openly putting forward the theory of "permanent revolution" which would install the communist vanguard in power by applying terror against the *petit-bourgeois* majority of the population.

In the West, where nascent industrialism was backed by centuries of capitalist experience and a great liberal humanistic-scientific culture, this theory was too crude to succeed. Marx realised this and stated, in September 1850, that its application should be suspended for an indeterminate time to allow appropriate cultural and organisational preparation.[5] To prevent the waiting from turning into praise for the *bourgeois* world, Marx spent the rest of his life trying to show against all evidence that this world was irremediably condemned and that, therefore, the hope of revolution should not be abandoned. Many years later, in 1881, when answering to a Dutch follower, Domela Nieuwenhuis, who wanted to know something more precise about the time of the revolution, Marx attributed to the theory of downfall a function similar to the Christian belief in the end of this world. It was to avoid the inevitable compromise with capitalism which obstinately survived and prospered, becoming a lasting arrangement instead of "provisional", an enthusiastic acceptance of what existed instead of a tactical move, which would imply a subsequent unconditional surrender of revolutionary forces.

Marx wrote as follows:

"The doctrinaire and necessarily fantastic programme of action for a revolution of the future only diverts one from the struggle of the present. The dream that the end of the world was near inspired the early Christians in their struggle with the Roman Empire and gave them confidence in victory. Scientific insight into the inevitable disintegration of the dominant order of the society continually proceeding before our eyes and the evergrowing fury into which the masses are lashed by the old ghostly governments, while at the same time the possible development of the means of production advances with gigantic strides — all this is a sufficient guarantee that the moment a real proletarian revolution breaks out the conditions (though these are certain not to be idyllic) of its immediately next *modus operandi* will be in existence."[6]

Evidently if this wait with arms grounded lasted for too long, the dogma of the end of capitalism might not prevent a reconciliation in substance, though not explicitly proclaimed, between the Marxist workers' movement and the liberal civilisation. What was needed were signs, one almost says "miracles", which would perpetuate the illusion that the waiting was not in vain. That is why Marx, who was opposed to the Paris Commune, defended it in public as a consequence and, at the same time, a new proof of the validity of Marxism.[7] But what was required more practically was that, outside the increasingly solid fortress of advanced capitalism, there should arise a Marxist power capable both of functioning as a detonator of the revolution in

Europe, and of exporting it there, if need be with arms, in the name of the international solidarity of the proletariat.

So from 1872 until his death, precisely when in Europe he was breaking with anarchists and jacobins because (as Engels revealed in 1893) they might have provoked problems with the police, Marx ranged himself in favour of Russian anarchists-populists against the Marxists on the grounds that an early revolution was more than probable under the Russian conditions. Nor was it simply a tactical move. When Zasulich asked him in 1881 whether the Marxists should watch with relief the dismantling of the rural commune by capitalism, which was beginning in Russia at that time, Marx uncovered without hesitation the populist depth of his thinking. He said that saving the commune was not only possible, if a revolution arrived in time to strangle Russian capitalism in its cradle, but also highly desirable from a socialist standpoint since — and here Marx uses the words of the American ethnologist Henry L. Morgan — "the 'new system' to which modern society tends 'will be a revival in a superior form of a socially archaic type' ." In this way, Marx concludes, preventive anti-capitalist revolution would make it possible in Russia to evolve the commune

> "as an element of regeneration of the Russian society and, simultaneously, of superiority over the countries still enslaved by the capitalist regime."[8]

And a year later, in the preface to the second Russian edition of the *Manifesto* Marx added:

> "If the Russian revolution becomes the signal for a proletarian revolution in the West, so that the two will supplement each other, then the present rural ownership of land in Russia could be used as the starting point for a development in the communist direction."[9]

Excluding the reference to the rural commune, the basis of which had been in the meantime irremediably eroded by capitalism, Lenin's taking of power in 1917 and foundation of the Comintern in 1919 followed lines which were in substance analogous to those embarked on by Marx. According to both, the subsequent move should have been the exportation of revolution to Europe on the points of the Red Army's bayonets. Both Marx and Lenin thought that in this way they could reabsorb the anarchic-jacobin deviation and to stand the revolutionary project on its feet instead of on its head. But in the summer of 1920, the Red Army was blocked under the walls of Warsaw, abandoned to its fate by the Western proletariat which refused to rise.

The failure of this surrogate revolution was a sign that the foundations of capitalist societies were even more solid than Marx and Lenin always suspected in their heart of hearts. Therefore, it was entirely natural that the Bolshevik experiment developed according to the extreme logic of the premises which had been the reason for its success in Russia. Thus it arrived through the phases of the New Economic Policy and socialism in one country, to the explicit national populism of the triumphant years of Stalin.[10]

Emotional appeal

The time has come to ask whether there is any link between the jacobin-nationalist impulses of Marx of the 1840s and his alignment with Russian populists of the 1870s, also profoundly imbued with jacobinism and anarchism, or is there an absolute vacuum, filled only by the doctrine of *Das Kapital*, which at the first glance seems completely antithetic. The answer is that the link is to be found in that doctrine of labour value which is the basic postulate of the whole of *Das Kapital*.

Sesardic has shown that, as an analytical tool for explaining the real movement of prices, labour value is a directly misleading concept. However, let us consider its emotional content, that is its ideological meaning. It is extremely simple and disruptive. If social riches are the exclusive fruit of manual labour, "measured by means of a pendulum clock", it follows that capital is "the theft of other people's labour", "unpaid labour", "dead labour", "objectified" in commodities. Such a way of seeing things is typical of peasant pre-capitalist societies, because when total riches tend to remain constant year in year out, the sudden enrichment of some is possible only when others are plundered.

Unfortunately for Marx, everything changed with capitalism. Entrepreneurial and scientific ability raised astronomically the productivity of manual labour, which allowed for the first time a progressive improvement for everybody, albeit at different rates. Marx was aware of this, so much so that in his *Grundrisse* he praised "the enormous civilizing influence of capital" and defined it, in total contradiction with his general views, as "objectified scientific ability".[11] The logic of such reasoning would have led Marx to preach loyalty to capitalism by the working classes. That is why he takes refuge again in the mystification of labour value in the hope that this will spur on the proletariat to rise so as to re-appropriate the (supposedly) ill-gotten profits.

The expedient could not work. But Marx's successors used the same labour value to explain the malfunction of Marxism without being constrained to repudiate the revolutionary prospective, but on the contrary to extend it for the first time to the whole world. I am referring to the theory of imperialism, which consists in transferring the category of labour value from the interpretation of relations between capitalista and proletarians within a single society, to the interpretation of relations between capitalist nations and proletarian nations in the whole world.

If the riches of England are the fruit of labour extorted by its capitalists from the working class, it is perfectly logical to consider the riches of the entire world, concentrated in the hands of a few nations, the fruit of labour extorted from the large mass of poorer countries by richer countries. Indeed, if by definition the rich are rich because they take away from the poor, there is no reason why this principle should not apply even more at the international level.

In a first phase, this widening of the labour value theory was understood by Marxists in a very limited sense. Thus the proletarians of poor countries were being exploited by capitalists of the rich countries, possibly in cahoots with the capitalists of the colonies, using the crumbs of this loot to corrupt the more combative members of their own working class. In this way, Marxists thought that capitalist productive relations would soon spread over the whole world until the *bourgeoisie* would confront an immense army of proletarians, again exasperated by rising immiserization, without any external peasant masses which could be exploited to pay for the corruption of the proletarians. This was a consolation for Marxists after the prophesies of their master had not come true. Capitalism escaped Marx's prediction solely by taking to the imperialist road which, however, would with mathematical certainty bring it back into desperate confrontation identical with the one it had previously avoided, except that there would then be no way out.

Since this version of the prophesy did not come true either, Marxists are led to put the theory of imperialism to its extreme consequences. Mao calls "proletarian" a revolution which is exclusively national-peasant. Lin Piao — whose teachings are taken up by various third-world enthusiasts of today — transforms the "class struggle' from a national into an international revolution and calls on the countryside to revolt against the metropolis, including the Soviet Union. With such metamorphoses Marxism has tried to impose itself on adverse circumstances by exploiting to the maximum its own genetic patrimony. The transformations currently administered in the two main Marxist parties of the West — the French Socialist Party of Mitterand and the Italian Communist Party of Natta — now lay siege to what is the main feature of the doctrine, namely anti-capitalism. At this juncture, what is in question is no longer yet another adjustment but a genetic mutation. Should this transformation succeed, Marxism will be abolished, possible preserving just the name, by the very people who are supposed to keep it up. If it does not, Marxism in the West may go towards its extinction, perhaps slowly but inexorably.

Violence — limited future for Marxism

In its third-world version, Marxism still has a future. But when it overcomes the phase of industrial take-off — an achievement in which no Marxist country has so far succeeded, not even China — the process of adaptation will approach its natural limit also in the third world. But everywhere the descending parabola of Marxism is destined to be much retarded because the Soviet Union is exceedingly interested in its survival and will remain so as long as its ruling class continues to believe that Marx's doctrine is the only source available to legitimize its own power.

As Sesardic has shown, Marxism is after all utopian. But the historical critique suggests that we are dealing with a utopia which is different from the utopia Marx ascribed to his predecessors and adversaries. Theirs was a utopia in a pure state, in the sense that for achieving its aim it relied exclusively on the trust it had in the intrinsic goodness of its own content. The ideal would come true — this is substantially what all utopian socialists believed. Indeed, it could not but come true — because it was *just* that it should come true. The splendour of the true and of the just — as soon as it was sufficiently proclaimed — would suffice to dissolve the falsity and the distortions of this world.

In other words, what non-Marxist socialism lacked was the doctrine of a scapegoat. They failed to propagate the conviction that wrong is incarnated in a determined class of persons — for Marx, the capitalists and their lackeys

— who are prepared to oppose with absolute intransigence the advent of the good until they are "liquidated". Utopian socialism was a utopia without "duplicity", so much so that its promoters could be subsumed under the definition which Machiavelli coined for Savonarola: prophets disarmed, and for this reason destined to failure from the beginning.

On the contrary, as we have seen, Marx's originality consists precisely in the duplicity which leads him to construct the pretext of science because this is required to direct and rationalise violence. Further, there is in Marx an acute perception of the destructive potential resulting from the frustration and rejection that the march of capitalist industrialisation must bring forth in the peasant masses and amongst the intellectuals of the areas swept by the revolutionary cyclone and especially of the areas only marginally affected by it. Together with this perception, there is in the heritage of Marx the indication to his followers that they should not hesitate to use this destructive potential to further their own will to power, even if this may sound contrary to the esoteric meaning of the doctrine. In Machiavelli's terms, Marxism should be defined as "armed prophesy" rather than as utopia. It is a formidable call to anti-capitalist and anti-liberal mobilisation, strengthened with the required instructions to make it come true. And it is for this reason that Marxism had at least a possibility of success which all the other utopias were lacking.

In the end, one must say that the results of the historical critique of Marxism do not only align themselves with the results of the theoretical critique; they merge with it and reinforce it. The historical critique shows why and how Marxism could succeed — as it has in effect succeeded — to take power over a large part of the earth's surface. But since it lacked a positive project for the organisation of the economy and the state — as emerges from the theoretical critique — its pretensions of scientific analysis were spoiled at the root by its revolutionary wishful thinking. As a result Marxism could not but descend, like an army of occupation upon a conquered society which is forced to feed its oppressors from its own lympth of life. Even worse, the occupied society is pushed to the brink of extinction as has happened more than once in Russia and, in a still more apocalyptic way, in Pol Pot's Cambodia.

FOOTNOTES

1. The Italian translation of the monumental work by Marek Waldenberg has precisely the title *The Red Pope.*
2. Zanardo A., 1977, p. 476. In fact, Lenin himself, when he had already broken with the "renegade Kautsky", wrote that before 1914 Kautsky "was a Marxist and many of his works and invaluable experiences would for always remain a model of Marxism.". (In Waldenberg, 1980, p.5)
3. Lefebvre, 1983, pp. 20 and 34.
4. Sweezy, 1983, p. 88.
5. For a comment and the apposite Marxian texts, see Chapter IV of Settembrini, 1975.
6. Marx-Engels, 1955, p. 338.

7. On Marx and the Paris Commune see the two books by Settembrini, both published in 1974, passim. In 1881, in his reply to Nieuwenhuis, Marx said the following about the Commune: "Perhaps you will refer me to the Paris Commune; but apart from the fact that this was merely the rising of a city under exceptional conditions, the majority of the Commune was in no wise socialist, nor could it be. With a modicum of common sense, however, it could have reached a promise with Versailles useful to the whole mass of the people — the only thing that could be reached at the time." (Marx-Engels, 1955, p. 338)

8. Marx-Engels, 1965, pp. 238 and 244.

9. Marx-Engels, 1965, p. 246.

10. These developments of Marxism are analysed and documented in Settembrini, 1983.

11. Marx, 1970, pp. 11 and 403.

Works Cited

Lefebvre H., 1983: *Abbandonare Marx?* (Abandon Marx?) Roma: Editori Riuniti.

Marx. K., 1970: *Lineamenti fondamentali della critica dell'economia politica.* (*Grundrisse* of a critique of political economy). Vol.II Firenze: La Nuova Italia.

Marx K. — Engels F., 1955: *Selected Correspondence.* Moscow: Progress Publishers.

Marx. K. — Engels F., 1965: *India Cina Russia.* (India, China, Russia). Milano: Il Saggiatore.

Settembrini D., 1974: *Due ipotesi per il socialismo in Marx ed Engels.* (Two hypotheses on Socialism in Marx and Engels). Bari: Laterza.

Settembrini D., 1974: *Socialismo e rivoluzione dopo Marx.* (Socialism and revolution after Marx). Napoli: Guida.

Settembrini D., 1975: *Il labirinto marxista.* (The Marxist Labyrinth). Milano: Rizzoli.

Settembrini D., 1983: *Una Idea alla conquista del mondo.* (An Idea conquers the world). Cosenza: Giordano.

Sweezy P., 1983: *Il marxismo e il futuro.* (Marxism and the future). Torino: Einaudi.

Waldenberg M., 1980: *Il Papa rosso Karl Kautsky.* (Karl Kautsky, the red pope). Roma: Editori Riuniti.

Zanardo A., 1977: *Il marxismo* in *Storia delle idee politiche, economiche e sociali.* (Marxism in History of political, social and economic ideas). Edited by L. Firpo. Vol. V. Torino: UTET.

Annexe

PARTY TELLS CHINESE
MARX'S IDEAS ARE OUTDATED

Peking (Reuter, AP) — China said yesterday that many of the ideas of Marx and Lenin were outdated and accused ideology specialists in the leadership of delaying progress.

The official *People's Daily* said Mr Deng Xiaping's reforms were being obstructed by some people who stuck rigidly to the teachings of Marx and Lenin instead of studying economic realities.

In a front-page leading article, the paper told them to look at facts and be quiet for the next three to five years. "It is already 101 years since Marx died, his works were written more than a century ago," it said.

"Some concepts were right at the time and afterwards the situation changed greatly. There were many things that Marx, Engels and Lenin did not experience or come in contact with.

"One cannot take a dogmatic attitude towards Marxism ... to take some theories out of Marx's works in order to limit the richness of contemporary life can only impede the development of history," the newspaper said.

Western diplomats said the article seemed to bear out rumours among Chinese officials that Mr Deng had banned all political campaigns that might impede China's economic development during the next five years.

One diplomat said the article was also a criticism of Mr Deng Liqun, the party's propaganda chief, who last year supported a campaign against "spiritual pollution" from abroad that was used by some leftists to attack current policies.

Mr Deng Xiaoping is famous for his pragmatic approach to economics, summed up by his saying that it does not matter whether a cat is black or white so long as it catches rats. The party has already argued against dogmatism.

The declaration was the latest sign of what foreign observers have called the party's slow methodical reinterpretation of basic, orthodox Communist principles.

"When they say things like this, they are clearly trying to find a theoretical justification for what they are doing," said another Western diplomat, "It goes beyond what they've said before in terms of directness."

Mr Deng's attempts to remould China's economy include encouraging private enterprise, wooing foreign investment and promoting competition.

Mr Deng, who emerged as senior leader two years after the death of Mao Tse-tung in 1976, has reversed most of Mao's radical exhortations.

The material quality of rural Chinese life has sharply increased under Mr Deng's direction, with many peasants multiplying their incomes, building new homes and buying television sets, washing machines, new clothes and other items.

Meanwhile, the Hong Kong newspaper *Ming Pao* reported Mr Hu Yaobag, the party chief as saying the Communist Party will vote 47 new members on to the Central Committee to avert a succession crisis in its ageing leadership.

The Times, 8 December 1984

CHINESE WRITER FACES 'PURGE' OVER ARTICLE
by HUGH DAVIES in Peking

An editorial writer on the *People's Daily* organ of the Chinese Communist party, appeared to be in trouble last night after official sources told foreign correspondents in Peking that an article written by him on Marxism was wrong.

The unsigned article, published on the front page last Friday, caused headlines in some Western newspapers, which carried an interpretation by one news agency that the party was saying for the first time that the thinking of Marx was obsolete.

In fact, the editorial said that some of Marx's ideas were outdated and should not be followed dogmatically, word for word. It amounted to a call to refine Marxism to fit the conditions in the world today rather than those of a century or more ago.

But, in places like Hongkong, where many of the inhabitants have been praying that Chinese Communism is being watered down, the story provoked articles such as one in the *South China Morning Post* suggesting that "something momentous" was happening in China.

As a result Chinese officials had to make it clear yesterday that the article was flawed because it had not sufficiently stressed the continuing importance of Marxist principles, which were still China's guiding ideology.

The move to balance the paper's remarks followed a rare front-page correction by the *People's Daily* of a key sentence in the editorial.

It altered the phrase "one cannot expect Marx and Lenin's works of their time to solve our problems of today" to read "to solve all our problems of today."

Chinese sources said the article on theory and practice was based on remarks by Hu Yaobang, party general secretary to provincial propaganda officials and jotted down by editors without an official text.

It seems likely that the author will follow in the steps of two other *People's Daily* staff who were recently "purged" for supporting the seemingly heretical view that there could be alienation under Communism.

The Daily Telegraph, 11 December 1984

CRCE is grateful to the Reuter's Agency and The Daily Telegraph for permission to re-print the above articles

DATE DUE

HIGHSMITH #45230

Printed
in USA